Beginner's Guide to
N Scale Model Railroading

BY RUSS LARSON
PUBLISHER  Model Railroader
Magazine

MODEL RAILROAD HANDBOOK NO.8

ART DIRECTOR: Lawrence Luser
ARTIST: Phil Kirchmeier

Cover photo: The *20th Century Limited* races along the Hudson River at Breakneck Mountain on its way to New York City. This scene is on an Ntrak module built by Dick Christianson and Gordon Odegard. Dick describes how to build this module in Chapter 14. Photo by A. L. Schmidt.

This book was first published in 1974 as *N Scale Primer*. This new edition has been extensively revised and updated and includes much new material.

 KALMBACH BOOKS

First printing, 1990. Second printing, 1992. Third printing, 1993. Fourth printing, 1995. Fifth printing, 1997.

Printed in the United States of America

Fig. 1-1. The Union Pacific Northern is one of those rarest of layouts, one that's finished. It's provided hours of operating fun for Jim Whitehead and his half-dozen operators.

This is N scale

You can enjoy model railroading in many ways. If your work involves dealing with people all day, you may be looking for solitude at the end of it. You can pursue this hobby at home by building a layout or module either by yourself or with family members. If you want to be with people in your leisure time, you can join a club or a national association.

Model railroaders choose a particular scale for many reasons. Some are practical considerations, like the space available for a layout. The small size of N scale models is a real selling point for many. Others without space restrictions still select N scale simply because they like it. Or they want to build a more realistic layout where the scenery dominates the trains, as in real life.

Modular railroading, called Ntrak, is another way to enjoy N scale. The beauty of modular railroading is that you only build a piece of a layout to certain standards. Then you take your module to an Ntrak event where it can be connected to others to form a complete operating layout. Local modular clubs often set up layouts in shopping malls or at model railroad shows where they enjoy running long trains and at the same time promoting the hobby. Modules built by people in different parts of the country have been brought together to form huge layouts for national conventions.

Building a module is a good way with a minimum investment to get a taste of each aspect of building a layout. Modular railroading started with N scale in 1973 and has now spread to all major scales. It's become so popular with N scalers that I've devoted two chapters of this book to the subject.

As you page through this book you will notice this hobby has many facets. There is benchwork to be constructed, track to be laid, wires to be soldered, scenery and structures to be built, and of course, trains to be operated. There is satisfaction to be derived by meeting the many challenges of model railroading. Few beginners will be familiar with all these areas or have the skills necessary to do a first-rate job on their first layout. Skills are learned only by trying new things. Satisfaction comes from successfully meeting challenges.

Model railroading can be a creative outlet. Although you may have to earn your living doing routine tasks, you can express yourself in this hobby. You can — and should — build your model railroad the way you want it to look. A mistake here won't jeopardize your career. No life and death decisions are involved. You won't get chewed out for

Fig. 1-2. Two award-winning N scale scratchbuilt models: A 2″-square abandoned house by Patricia Ford and Hillcrest Lumber's Climax geared locomotive No. 9. by Phil Magnall (the motor, gears, and wheels are the only ready-made parts).

being slow or sloppy. If you are satisfied with what you are doing, and you are having a good time doing it, that's all that really matters.

Model railroading actually is several hobbies tied together by the objective of creating a realistic miniature railroad. Model railroaders heighten their enjoyment of the hobby by striving to create as convincing an impression of a real railroad as is possible in a small space.

To achieve this objective of building a complete layout, you should avoid two pitfalls:

1. Trying to do too much at first.
2. Refusing to try new things.

A few words of caution may help you avoid pitfall Number 1. Start small. It's as simple as that. Build your first layout small and uncomplicated, but do a complete job, including scenery. This way you will get a taste of each step in the process without having to do so much that you become discouraged. As this first layout takes form, you will learn the finer points of model railroading through practical experience which, in the last analysis, is still the best teacher. As questions arise, you will be searching through model railroad magazines and books for answers and asking friends in the hobby for advice.

As you learn more about the hobby you undoubtedly will get ideas for new features you'd like to have on your layout. You will be able to incorporate many of these features into your first layout through modifications or additions. After a period of time, you will accumulate a list of features that can't be added to the first layout. When you reach this point, it is time to plan a second and more ambitious layout — one that reflects your new level of model railroading know-how.

The second pitfall in building a comprehensive layout is refusing to try something new. This is the age of specialization. Although this may be desirable in industry, it is not always wise for a person to be a specialist in his hobby. Each person will like some areas of the hobby more than others, and his layout is bound to reflect this. However, the person who forever restricts his layout to a 4 x 8-foot sheet of plywood because he is afraid to tackle simple benchwork is cheating himself out of a lot of fun. Go ahead and try! What have you got to lose?

A large portion of this book is devoted to making the various steps in building a model railroad as easy as possible. I hope this book will help many newcomers to N scale model railroading overcome their hesitancy to try something new.

What to expect

What can you expect to derive from this hobby? You can expect to learn new skills, overcome challenges, possibly discover latent talent, and, most

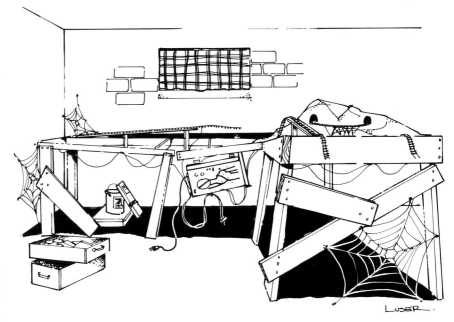

Fig. 1-3. Many beginners make the mistake of trying to do too much too soon.

important, have an enjoyable time in the process.

The only person you have to satisfy in this hobby, or in any hobby for that matter, is yourself. If you are satisfied with what you're doing, it doesn't matter what anyone else thinks; if you are not satisfied, no amount of praise will help.

Go ahead and try each phase of this exciting hobby. Try to do the best you can, but above all else have fun.

Modeling scales

Scale is the proportion between the model and its prototype. This book is devoted to the modeling ratio of 1:160. Whenever I refer to this proportion, the term "N scale" will be used.

Two other modeling ratios are popular: 1:48 proportion (O scale), and 1:87 proportion (HO scale). See fig. 1-5. Modeling also is done in proportions of 1:64 (S scale), 1:220 (Z scale), and G scale, which varies.

HO is the most popular modeling scale and many people are familiar with its size. A size comparison of the two scales will help many readers develop a "feel" for N scale. N scale models are 54.5 percent as large as HO models (1/160 divided by 1/87). This means an N scale layout can be built in an area which is approximately 30 percent as large as that required for a comparable HO layout. Stated another way, you can build 3.3 times as big an N scale railroad in any given area.

Fig. 1-4. Some modelers fall into a rut and refuse to experience other hobby facets.

Fig. 1-5. The three most popular modeling ratios: 1:160 (N scale), left; 1:87 (HO scale), center; and 1:48 (O scale), right.

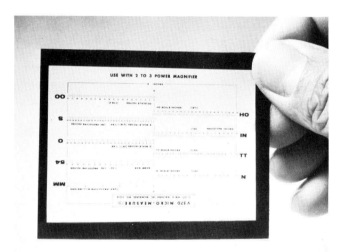

Fig. 1-6. The Micro-Measure, sold by Wm. K. Walthers, Inc., of Milwaukee, Wisconsin, can be used to make N scale measurements as small as 1 scale inch.

Fig. 1-7. Although the N scale Berkshire locomotive shown in the bottom does not contain all details shown in the prototype above, the overall effect of realism is good.

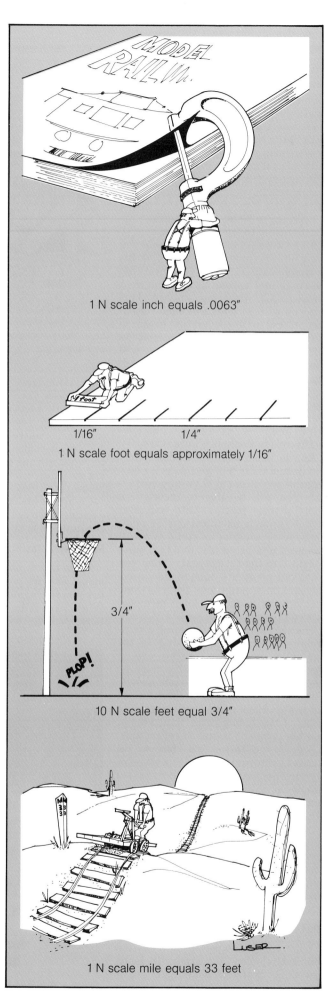

1 N scale inch equals .0063″

1 N scale foot equals approximately 1/16″

10 N scale feet equal 3/4″

1 N scale mile equals 33 feet

Richard Steinheimer.

Fig. 1-8. "Gauge" is the distance between rail heads, measured from inside to inside. Standard prototype gauge is 4'-8½".

Scaling down prototype dimensions

If we divide 12″ by 160, we find that 1′ in N scale equals 0.075″. The N scale equivalent of any dimension can be found by dividing by 160. The N Scale Conversion Table on page 5 will save lots of tedious arithmetic.

Long division or the conversion table need be used only for making very exact measurements. There are N scale rules available which enable the modeler to measure directly in scale feet, thereby eliminating the conversion. The scale rule printed along the edge of this page can be cut out, mounted on a strip of cardstock, and used temporarily until you can purchase a metal one at your hobby shop. The majority of rules are divided into 6″ scale increments. Wm. K. Walthers, Inc., sells a measuring tool called the Micro-Measure which enables you to make measurements as small as 1 scale inch. See fig. 1-6.

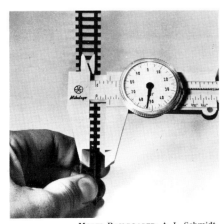

MODEL RAILROADER: A. L. Schmidt.

Fig. 1-9. An N scale model of standard-gauge track has a track gauge of 9 millimeters, which is equal to .354″.

Scale models

Strictly speaking, every part (and every detail on every part) of a scale model should be an exact miniature replica of the prototype. See fig. 1-7. It would appear then that to build a perfect N scale model merely would be a matter of getting the prototype dimension drawings and reducing all sizes to 1/160. If such an approach were practical, all our models would, indeed, be perfect. In reality this is not the case. Total authenticity is rarely achieved even in the larger modeling scales. Certain compromises are inevitable. Here are some of the reasons for this.

There is a practical limit to the fineness of detail that can be modeled, even under a magnifying glass. Therefore some of the very small parts on the prototype must be made oversize or simply left out. Notice in the N Scale Conversion Table that 2½″ in N scale is equal to only ¹/₆₄″.

A model built for display purposes may have finer detail than one intended to be operated on a model railroad. Models of locomotives and other rolling stock must be rugged enough to hold up under normal use. Consequently, some parts must be made oversize for strength.

Most N scale equipment is produced on high-speed plastic molding equipment. Production problems enter into the design of the master model to some extent. Fortunately, the state of the art has advanced to the point where few serious compromises are necessary.

Certain industry standards must be followed in the manufacture of track, wheels, and couplers, so that one manufacturer's equipment will be compatible with all others. The original standards for these items were established more for reliable operation than for appearance. Hence, the track, wheels, and couplers are the most out-of-scale items on an N scale layout.

The overall effect

I've mentioned just a few of the reasons models in general, and N scale models in particular, are not 100 percent to scale. You should be aware of this and be on the lookout for ways to improve the authenticity of your models. The overall effect is really what is important. Does the model, when viewed as a whole, bear a reasonable resemblance to the prototype? Are enough significant details included so that this model is not confused with models of similar prototypes? As you become more involved in this hobby, you'll be able to spot a good model right away. Start looking for the subtle points which distinguish outstanding models from mediocre ones.

Track gauges

"Gauge" is the distance between the

N SCALE CONVERSION TABLE			
Prototype dimension in inches	N scale equivalent dimension in inches	Prototype dimension in inches/feet	N scale equivalent dimension in inches
¹/₆₄	.0001	4¼	.02656
¹/₃₂	.00019	4½	.02812
¹/₁₆	.00039	5	.03125
⅛	.00078	5¼	.03281
¼	.00156	5½	.03437
⅜	.00234	6	.0375
½	.00312	6¼	.03906
⅝	.0039	6½	.04062
¾	.00468	7	.04375
⅞	.00546	8	.05
1	.00625	9	.05625
1⅛	.00703	10	.0625
1¼	.00781	11	.06875
1⅜	.00859		
1½	.00937		
1⅝	.01015	1'	.075
1¾	.01093	2'	.15
1⅞	.01171	3'	.225
2	.0125	4'	.30
2¼	.01406	5'	.375
2½	.01562	6'	.45
3	.01875	7'	.525
3¼	.02031	8'	.60
3½	.02187	9'	.675
4	.025	10'	.75

Here's an example of how to use this table. Find the N scale equivalent of 5'6-¹⁵/₁₆".

Prototype	5'0	= .375″ in N scale
	6″	= .0375″
	⅞″	= .00546″
	¹/₁₆″	= .00039″
5'6-¹⁵/₁₆″		= .41835″

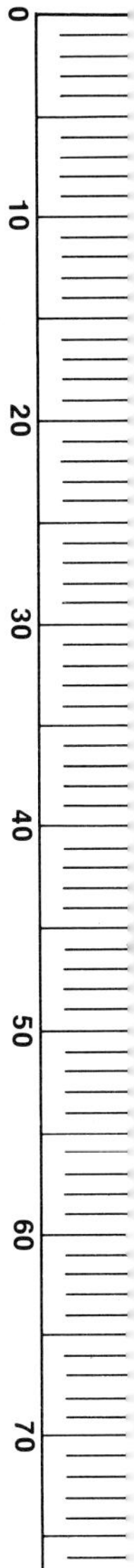

rails, measured from inside to inside. Standard prototype rail gauge is 4'8½". See fig. 1-8. However, many railroads were built with a rail spacing less than the standard. These were called narrow-gauge railroads. The most common of the narrow gauges in this country were 2 feet and 3 feet. To designate the gauge being modeled list the scale, then a small letter "n" followed by the gauge. A 3-foot narrow-gauge railroad modeled in HO scale is written HOn3. Modeling narrow-gauge railroads is popular in HO and O scales, but is rare in N scales. Equipment is available — Nn3 freight cars by Kadee and steam loco bodies from Gold Rush Models which fit on Marklin Z scale mechanisms.

A scale model of standard-gauge track in 1:160 proportion is equal to 4'8½" divided by 160, or 9 millimeters. Nine-millimeter track gauge is referred to as N gauge in this book. This is usually given in millimeters, because the pioneering work in N scale was done in Europe where the meter is the standard unit of length. Nine millimeters is equal to .354". See fig. 1-9.

N Scale Rule

0
10
20
30
40
50
60
70
80
90
100

Fig. 2-1. This San Jose Society of Model Railroaders' pike is a good example of a layout whose elements are all in harmony with each other.

Planning your railroad

Fig. 2-2. Your model railroad must have an economic reason for existence. Plan to include a number of "customers" on your layout such as this industry.

Concept to completion

A model railroad is more than track, roadbed, buildings, tunnels, mountains, and roads. These are the elements we see, but more important is the concept that brought these elements together in a harmonious manner.

The layout concept is the main factor that distinguishes scale model railroading from simply "playing with toy trains." Developing a concept for your model railroad is part of the fun. This is your chance to be creative. You decide the what, where, why, and how of this project.

Your initial plan does not have to be worked out to the last detail; remember, you're in this hobby for enjoyment. However, there are three things you should decide before you start actual construction:

• The economic reason for the railroad's existence.

• The historical setting of the railroad.

Fig. 2-3. Select equipment in agreement with the historical setting of your railroad. The old-time passenger train is by Rapido; the Amtrak by Con-Cor.

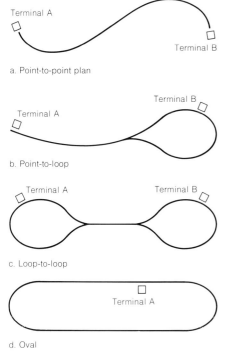

a. Point-to-point plan

b. Point-to-loop

c. Loop-to-loop

d. Oval

Fig. 2-4 BASIC CONFIGURATIONS

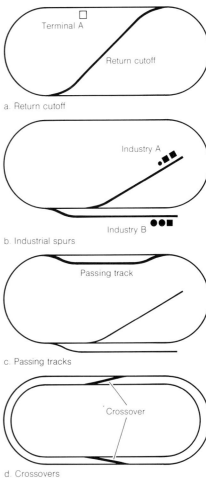

a. Return cutoff

b. Industrial spurs

c. Passing tracks

d. Crossovers

Fig. 2-5

The historical setting

Railroads have been around a long time — beginning in the 1830s. Progress throughout this long history has been constant. Today's railroads have little in common with those railroads of 140 years ago. Because there have been so many changes, you must specify a time setting for your model railroad so that you can select model locomotives, passenger cars, freight cars, buildings, scenery, and other equipment that are consistent with the era you've chosen.

Currently, the largest selection of N scale equipment is of the modern type and, generally speaking, the farther back in time you decide to place your railroad, the smaller your selection of equipment becomes.

The geographical setting

Select a geographical location for your layout that you are familiar with, so you can design and build realistic scenery. Make sure that your intended revenue sources, such as mines or logging operations, are the type which would be found in your chosen geographic area.

Both the geographic and historic settings must be considered when you select structures for the layout.

The track plan

Before starting to build a layout in any given space, be it a 2 x 4-foot sheet of plywood or a basement empire, you will be better off if you work out a track plan in detail. You have the choice of either using a published plan or designing one of your own. Whichever you choose, there are some fundamentals of track planning you should know.

Basic configurations — In prototype railroading, trains run from one terminal to another and back again, stopping at stations in between. A model railroad track plan that is arranged in this manner is a point-to-point system. See fig. 2-4a. If you add a return loop at one terminal, it becomes a point-to-loop system. See fig. 2-4b. Two loops, one at each end, make it a loop-to-loop plan, as in fig. 2-4c. The loops often are folded back over one another to fit the track into a smaller space or to gain more mileage. Oval track plans and

• The geographical setting of the railroad.

Once established, these three guidelines will help you to build a layout with all elements in reasonable harmony.

An economic reason for existence

Railroad companies transport goods from place to place for profit. The people and companies the railroad serves are its customers. Your model railroad must have "customers" to serve as well. There must be stations, and factories, mines, mills, and other sources of revenue on the layout. Of course, there is a practical limit to the number of customers you can include on your layout. However, even the smallest model railroad must have some customers to justify its existence.

The financial condition of your railroad also should be established. This affects the overall appearance of the layout. A prosperous company would operate new equipment and all of its structures would be in good repair, whereas a company on the verge of bankruptcy would be getting by with old decrepit equipment.

loop-to-loop plans provide for nonstop operation of trains. This can make the main line seem longer, since you can run a train around two complete circuits, for example, before it returns to the station. With oval plans you often have just one terminal, as in fig. 2-4d. You run your train around the oval once or twice and imagine that it is arriving at a different terminal. You may vary the oval plan by adding a return cutoff track as shown in fig. 2-5a. The train can be turned on this track so it comes back into the station from a different direction.

Industrial spurs — An otherwise simple plan may be improved by adding industrial spurs as shown in fig. 2-5b. Most published track plans include several spurs, but you might want to add more, or rearrange them. It is not necessary to follow the plans exactly when laying spur tracks.

Passing tracks — Should you want to run more than one train at a time, as most modelers do, you will have to make provisions for trains to pass each other. You do this by adding a passing siding. See fig. 2-5c. If one train overtakes a slower one, route the slower one into the passing siding to permit the faster train to pass. Plan to include as many passing tracks as you have trains, preferably more. A passing siding at a yard can function as a run-around track as well.

Crossovers — If you have a double-track main line, the trains going in opposite directions need never meet each other head on. You should have a pair of crossovers between mainline tracks so a slow train can pull onto the "wrong main" to let a fast train pass. You need the second crossover so the train can be routed back onto "right main" again without having to back up. See fig. 2-5d.

Yards — There are two basic types of yard track arrangements: *stub* and *through* as illustrated in fig. 2-6. The stub yard often is used because it is cheaper to build (it requires fewer turnouts) and it provides numerous operating opportunities for the small pike. A stub yard also can hold more cars than the through type, because less space is used for turnouts.

Runaround tracks — These are essential in railroading, both prototype and model. You need them if you intend to do much yard or industrial switching. Figure 2-7 shows that the runaround track allows the locomotive of a train to uncouple, proceed around the train to the rear, and push cars into a stub-end track without becoming trapped. This track can be a crossover between two yard or mainline tracks, or it can be a passing siding.

Track plans

The easiest approach to track planning is to select a published track plan that fits the space available.

Many good track-plan books are sold at your local hobby shop and new ones are constantly being published by the model railroad magazines. The more detailed plans include a table of dimensions for each gauge.

Select a plan designed to fit a space smaller than the space you have available. This will allow a margin for error — a critical consideration with track plans for small spaces. After all, you do not have room at one end of the layout to correct a mistake made at the other end.

In addition to using a published track plan, you can develop your own track plan. There are two basic approaches to original track planning. One is to scale down an actual railroad operation and the other is to dream up a fictional railroad operation that could have existed somewhere.

If you are scaling down a plan you're interested in that was designed for HO or a larger scale, keep in mind that the aisle spacing cannot be scaled down. The space needed for two train operators to pass one another remains constant.

In reality, it is almost impossible to build an exact scale model of even a small portion of a real railroad in a practical-size space. What you can do,

however, is look for interesting features that lend themselves to modeling. Begin by taking a look at the railroad operations in your area. Perhaps there is a freight office, a scale house, a feed mill, a lumber company, or some other railroad structure that would fit into your plan. Then observe the trackage. Is there something interesting such as a turntable, wye, street trackage, or sidings with steep grades that you would like to duplicate?

After selecting some features from a prototype railroad, you will have to incorporate them into your plan in a way that captures the flavor of the prototype. Methods of doing this have been described many times in MODEL RAILROADER's "Railroad you can model" articles. I'd suggest you read some of these articles to learn how others have transferred a real railroad operation into a similar scale model railroad operation.

Many modelers dream up their own railroad to model. This approach can be more fun for those who have a fertile imagination and know enough about prototype railroad operation to develop a convincing model operation. This method allows you to combine features you like about several real railroads located in different parts of the country (or the world for that matter) with scenery from your favorite area and enables you to operate your railroad as you think a railroad should be operated.

To illustrate the fictional approach to track planning, I developed a story about the Riverport Railway & Navigation Co. Even if you work from a published plan, you may want to invent your own story and name. This is part of the fun and it helps you to keep all of the elements of the layout in agreement.

Riverport Railway & Navigation Co.

Riverport began as a small trading center for settlers who lived near the junction of the Crooked and Rock rivers. The Rock River was heavily traveled, with several large cities located upstream from Riverport.

Farmersville, located 14 miles upstream from Riverport on the Crooked River, also was a trading center. A trading post was established there in 1857 by Zeke Crocker. Zeke hauled his goods upstream from Riverport on barges pulled by mules. His business thrived as more and more homesteaders settled on the rich farmland in the area.

As Farmersville prospered, a road was built along the river to provide a faster means of transportation to meet the demands of the people.

In 1890 a rich vein of lead was discovered in the foothills of the Molehill mountain range near Farmersville. The local entrepreneur, Cash Hart, considered building a railroad between his mine and the Crooked River. This would enable him to ship the ore to the

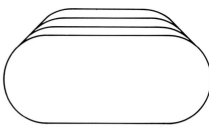

a. Through yard

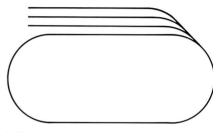

b. Stub yard

Fig. 2-6 YARDS

river where it would be loaded onto barges and shipped downstream to a smelter he planned to build at Riverport. However, before constructing the railroad, he offered to build his smelter in Farmersville if the townspeople would finance the building of a railroad between the mine and Farmersville. This arrangement not only would save Hart the cost of building the railroad, but would cut his operating cost by eliminating barge loading/unloading.

Zeke Crocker and other local businessmen wanted the smelter built at Farmersville. They formed a company and financed the railroad construction with the understanding that the Hart Mine would operate the line at its expense.

The Hart Mine prospered and so did Farmersville. This new wealth placed an additional strain on the river and overland transportation routes between the two towns.

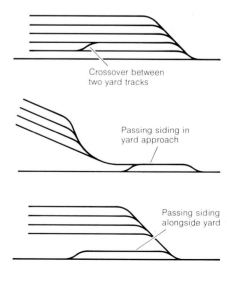

Crossover between two yard tracks

Passing siding in yard approach

Passing siding alongside yard

Fig. 2-7 RUNAROUND TRACKS

Fig. 2-8. Many modelers dream up their own railroad to model: "In 1910 the main line of the Consolidated Railroad was completed through Riverport..."

In 1899 the Zeke Crocker Navigation Co., which operated the river barges and held controlling interest in the railroad to the Hart Mine, constructed a railroad between Farmersville and Riverport to handle the increasing freight business. The company was renamed the Riverport Railway & Navigation Co. at the insistence of the Riverport State Bank which financed the project. The RR&NC purchased the rolling stock operated by the Hart Mine and contracted to handle all its freight operations.

With business flourishing, Riverport looked like an attractive rail connection for the Consolidated Railroad, which was planning a new east-west main line through the area. In 1910 the main line of the Consolidated Railroad was completed through Riverport. A small interchange yard and a combina-

tion freight and passenger station were constructed by Consolidated. Riverport Railway & Navigation Co. was hooked into the vast U. S. rail network.

Traffic on the RR&NC remained fairly constant over the years with steady but not exceptional growth. The barge operations of the company ended when the connection was made with Consolidated.

Consolidated offered passenger service to Riverport until Amtrak took over passenger service on May 1, 1971. Its main line through Riverport was not included in the Amtrak network.

Now that we have the history of a railroad that might have been and we have a map of the imaginary area it served, we can develop our model railroad from them. First, let's see if it is practical to build an exact N scale replica of this fictional short line.

Space required — The area shown on the map, fig. 2-9, is 10 miles long and 6 miles wide. An N scale model of this area would result in a layout 330 feet long and 198 feet wide — clearly an impossible task!

The towns — A scale model of the town of Riverport alone would be 33 feet square. It would be impossible to include all the buildings in an exact scale model of a town of 5000 people. Assuming a typical population density of 3.5 people per household, a town of 5000 would have about 1400 homes, plus a business district.

Scenery — Molehill Mountain rises to a height of 2000 feet in the upper left-hand corner of the area shown on the map. An exact scale model of even a small mountain like this would equal 12½ feet in N scale.

These figures demonstrate that it would be virtually impossible to build an exact N scale model of this short line railroad. However, we can build a model railroad that captures the flavor of the Riverport Railway & Navigation Co. if we carefully select what should be included and what should be excluded. Let us look again at the three essential elements of a layout and examine how they apply to the Riverport Railway & Navigation Co.

An economic reason for existence — On the RR&NC freight business runs between the mine and the smelter and also the two towns. The essential economic elements are the mine, the smelter, a station at each town, and several factories.

The historical setting — From the history of the RR&NC we know that the first track was laid in 1890 between the mine and the smelter. The track between the two towns was completed in 1899. Within these limits, the time setting of the layout is up to the modeler.

The geographical setting of the railroad — The exact part of the country was not specified but we do know something about the area. Two rivers cut through this area and both are important to the history of these towns. There is also part of a low mountain range which contains deposits of lead. Farming in this river valley is good; this is why people settled here. The rivers and the mountains should be included in a model railroad layout.

Space, time, and money — The essential elements of this railroad can be used as the basis for many track plans of various sizes and shapes. The larger the layout, the more authentic a replica of the prototype can be modeled. See fig. 2-11.

Begin the track plan by outlining the area you have available for the layout. A scale of 3 inches to 1 foot is a convenient one to use for N scale. First locate the curves and then arrange the rest of the mainline track. Then add passing tracks, yards, and the remaining track-

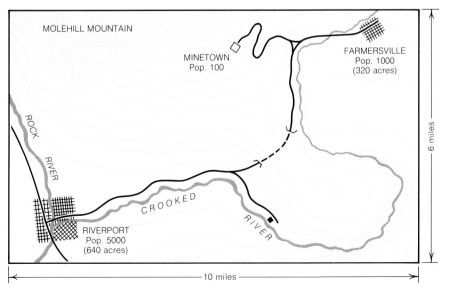

Fig. 2-9. This is the area served by the RR&NC. It's impractical to build an exact scale model of an area this large, but it is possible to capture its flavor.

age. Several sheets of paper later, and after wearing out an eraser or two, you should arrive at a design that you are satisfied with.

There are several dimensions to keep in mind while drawing your track plan: turnout size, minimum curve radius, minimum track separation to avoid side-swiping, clearances for trackside structures, maximum grades, and overhead clearances. This reference data is presented in fig. 2-10. In addition, templates for various makes of turnouts and crossings in a scale size of 3 inches to 1 foot can be found in many model railroading magazines and books. This information should enable you to design any type of N scale model railroad.

Remember that any track plan can be changed after it is put on paper — don't think you cannot add or subtract a section here and there if you choose. Most model railroaders let a new track plan design sit on the shelf a while before beginning construction. When they pick it up again, it is like taking a critical look at someone else's work. They can see improvements they would like to make here and there. Such changes are much easier to make with an eraser than with a hammer and chisel.

Scenery is part of the plan

All of the work you put into a model railroad has one objective — to create a lifelike setting in which model trains operate. Believable scenery is necessary to achieve this objective. To be credible, scenery must be developed in conjunction with the track plan. It should not be added as an afterthought. Although minor scenic details can be added later, the locations of the major elements such as mountains, rivers, towns, and large industries require planning.

Prototype railroads have to adapt their track routes to the terrain they pass through. In model railroading the scenery should give the observer the impression that the track route was planned through the scenery. There should be a scenic reason for every curve and grade on the layout.

An easy conclusion for a beginner to reach is that you must be an artist to create realistic-looking scenery. This is *not* true. You do have to develop a sensitivity for color, fitness, and proportion. Careful observation of the scenery around you will develop this sensitivity. Simply step outdoors and you will be standing in your "classroom" and looking at the best "textbook" on the subject.

If you have ever taken a cross-country train or automobile trip you undoubtedly have observed an important geological fact which will help you create realistic scenery: Transitions take place slowly. You never see an arid desert next to a deep pine forest, for example.

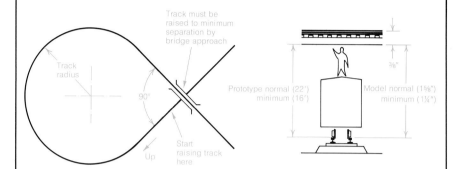

OVERPASS LOOP GRADES		
	GRADE	
Radius	(1⅝") Minimum separation	(2") Normal separation
8"	3.0%	3.7%
9"	2.7%	3.3%
10"	2.4%	3.0%
11"	2.2%	2.7%
12"	2.0%	2.5%
14"	1.7%	2.1%
16"	1.5%	1.9%
18"	1.4%	1.7%

KEY PLANNING DATA	
Proportion from prototype	1/160
Scale foot in actual inches	.075"=1 foot
Standard track gauge	.354"
Minimum track radius	7½"
Minimum track center-to-center separation	1¼"
Separation of tracks at overhead crossings	2"
Clearance from top of rail to underside of bridge or structure	1⅝"
Clearance from center of straight track to structures at side	⅝"

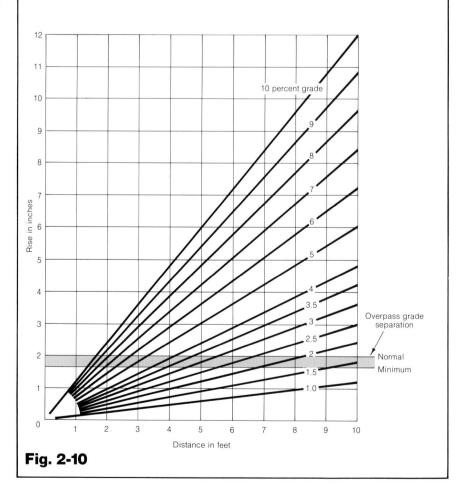

Fig. 2-10

Sometimes you may have to resort to more abrupt changes on your layout because of space limitations. Make them as gradual as possible, though. This will go a long way toward achieving a realistic-looking model railroad.

A chapter is devoted entirely to scenery later in the book (Chapter 9, Scenery made simple). I wanted to emphasize the importance of early scenery planning now before you decide on your track plan.

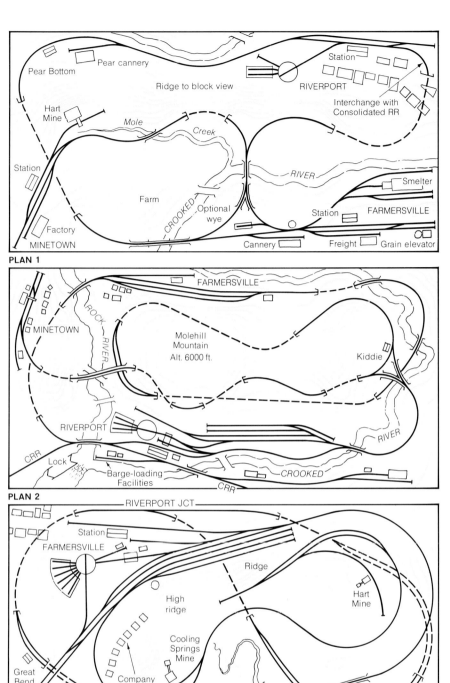

PLAN 1

PLAN 2

PLAN 3

Fig. 2-11. Plan 1 is an uncrowded layout with opportunity for both point-to-point and continuous running. Plan 2 also allows continuous running and lets you try your hand at building bridges and mountains. Plan 3 has room for two people to operate at once, one on the main line and the other on the branch to the mines.

Putting your scenery ideas on paper

When you are satisfied with the plan, make a scenic overlay with transparent paper and sketch in rivers, mountains, and other scenic effects you plan to include. Make several of these overlays until you arrive at just what you want. It's better to use up a little paper now than to be dissatisfied later.

Track plans based on the RR&NC

I asked two Kalmbach staff members to each sketch a track plan based on

the story of the Riverport Railway & Navigation Co. Plans 1 and 2 of fig. 2-11 are the result. In addition, Plan 3 was adapted from a plan that was published some years ago in MODEL RAILROADER.

A 4 x 8-foot sheet of plywood provides enough space for a good-sized layout, yet it is small enough for one man to build and maintain. Each of these three plans would make a layout that would keep you busy and happy for several years.

The first two plans follow the RR&NC story closely, but the third, a modification of a plan by John Armstrong published in the November 1953 issue of MODEL RAILROADER, takes the story further.

The high-quality lead ore produced by the Hart Mine attracted notice, and in the 1920s the Python Brass Company purchased the mine and the railroad. Python's geologists explored the Molehill Range and discovered another deposit of lead between Farmersville and Minetown. Not long afterwards the Cooling Springs Mine was making withdrawals from that deposit. The new mine added revenue to the railroad and taxed the capacity of the smelter at Farmersville. Python consolidated its smelting activities at another plant beyond Riverport, and the RR&NC became a heavy ore carrier, like the Duluth, Missabe & Iron Range. Ore cars became the predominant type of rolling stock.

Prototype ore cars are about 25 feet long. Ore is so heavy that, were the cars much longer, the extra volume of ore they could carry would exceed the capacity of two four-wheel trucks. In other words, the weight of the load in an ore car is about the same as the weight of the load in an 86-foot-long auto-parts box car.

Since the unit of measure for ore cars is more often "dozen" than "each," you may want to permanently couple your ore cars in cuts of four or six with drawbars made of brass or styrene. It will reduce the number of couplers you need, if you should convert to Kadees, and it will permit prototypical close coupling.

Operation on Plan 3 could keep many people busy. One switcher, a chunky 0-6-0 or 0-8-0 (somehow this railroad seems to be a steam one), could handle the task of taking empties to the mines and bringing back loads, while another could shuffle cars and build trains in the yard at Farmersville. The main line calls for at least a 2-8-2, and the curves, which are adequate for HO scale, could easily accommodate a 2-8-8-2. Don't neglect passenger service. A daily round trip or two with a 4-6-2, a baggage-mail car, and a coach would be appropriate for this type of railroad. A through sleeper from Chicago (or wherever), perhaps painted the colors of the connecting railroad, would give the Python management a simple way to reach the Farmersville branch of the company.

The layout is complete as it is, but it would be an easy matter to add a branch extending from any of the corners of the layout to serve an agricultural area. Additionally, there is room in the two right-hand corners of the layout for an industry of some kind, if you should decide you want more switching opportunities.

EMD diesels thunder through the Tehachapi Mountains on Jim Kelly's N scale version of the Southern Pacific's Mojave subdivision. The SP train is headed by a pair of Key SD40T-2s and a Con-Cor SD40-2. Two Hallmark SD40-2s and a Model Power SD45 head the Santa Fe train. The scenic highlight of Jim's layout is SP's famous Tehachapi Loop.

H. D. Morgan Jr. photo

"Easy does it" is the watchword when a White River & Naches crew switches the Swauk Crushed Rock Co. on Walter R. Naff's free-lance 11' x 14' layout set in Washington state. This is sure no place to put a car on the ground.

Along the N scale right of way

It's one of those blistering July days when you can hear the corn growing. The crew of Chicago, Burlington & Quincy no. 5629 is getting ready for the evening run to collect the milk being produced in barns across western Illinois. Roger Carlson of White Bear Lake, Minnesota, built and photographed this N scale diorama. The water tank, shanty, and figures are Bachmann. The coaling tower was built from a Heljan kit and the locomotive is a Rivarossi light Pacific. Roger weathers all his structures and equipment with acrylic paints.

Wayne and Bill Reid of suburban Chicago have built one of the finest N scale layouts in the country. Their Cumberland Valley System is based on four prototype railroads that operated in this part of Pennsylvania in the 1950s. (Above) On this steam-to-diesel transition era railroad we see a diesel-powered freight passing Greencastle on its way to Shippensburg while a steam locomotive switches cars at local industries. (Below) Running eastward toward Harrisburg, a Pennsy local freight curves around the base of Green Mountain. The Cumberland Valley System derives much of its realism from the way its scenery dominates the trains. Both photos were taken by Art Schmidt.

MODEL RAILROADER: A. L. Schmidt.

Fig. 3-1. Before the track, the wiring, and the scenery must come the benchwork, the supporting structure for the railroad. L-girder benchwork such as this is much sturdier than its spindly appearance implies.

Build a firm foundation

Prototype considerations

When a railroad company decided to join two communities by rail, it sent a surveying team to chart the best route. The company had to consider both the immediate cash outlay for purchase of right of way and construction costs as well as the long-term operating expense.

The ideal route would allow the railroad's locomotives to pull the heaviest loads at the highest speeds.

The roadbed for such a railroad would be level and straight. However, level and straight roadbeds often were impossible to build over any distance because of such natural obstacles as mountains, valleys, lakes, and rivers.

On the other hand, the cheapest railroad that could be built was one that followed the natural contour of the land as much as possible and avoided the serious obstacles by going around them. A few circuitous routes with steep grades were built but tonnage and speed on such railroads were limited.

Most railroads chose a compromise between the ideal and the least expensive. Grades were kept to a minimum but some ups and downs were inevitable. Curves, bridges, trestles, and tunnels often were necessary.

To achieve a credible job of modeling the railroads, grades as well as curves, fills, cuts, bridges, trestles, and tunnels must be included. Our roadbed should go uphill, downhill, through mountains, across rivers and marshes — wherever prototype railroads go. It is not necessary that a model railroad include all these elements, but when planning your model railroad, consider including those elements that real railroads employed in the same geographical setting. A realistic railroad will definitely be more difficult to model but the result will be worth all the extra ef-

Frederick H. Miller.

Fig. 3-2. Tunnels and cuts provide an easy railroad grade through mountainous terrain.

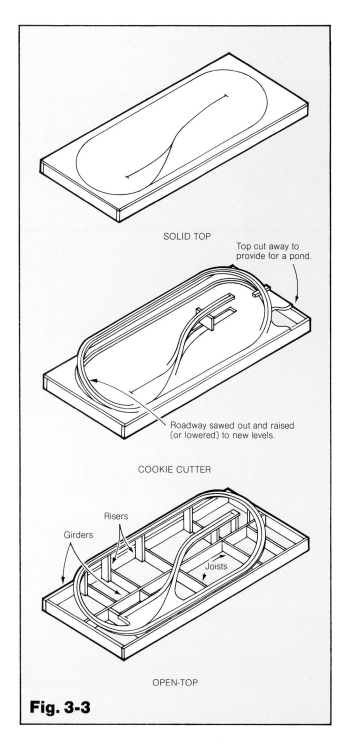

SOLID TOP

Top cut away to provide for a pond.

Roadway sawed out and raised (or lowered) to new levels.

COOKIE CUTTER

Girders

Risers

Joists

OPEN-TOP

Fig. 3-3

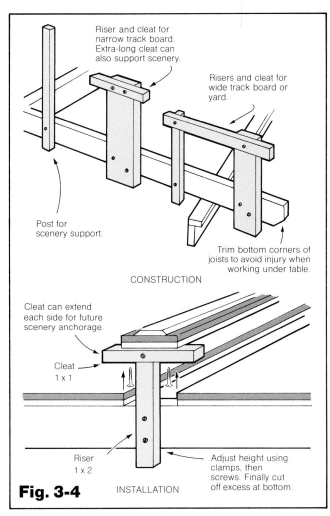

Riser and cleat for narrow track board. Extra-long cleat can also support scenery.

Risers and cleat for wide track board or yard.

Post for scenery support.

Trim bottom corners of joists to avoid injury when working under table.

CONSTRUCTION

Cleat can extend each side for future scenery anchorage.

Cleat 1 x 1

Riser 1 x 2

Adjust height using clamps, then screws. Finally cut off excess at bottom.

Fig. 3-4 INSTALLATION

Fig. 3-5. Spline-lattice roadbed is strong and economical.

fort. After all, the simplest railroad to model would be one with all track on a flat surface, and no bridges, trestles, or tunnels. Such a model railroad, however, suffers from a lack of authenticity and isn't very interesting.

Common types of benchwork

N scale layouts can be wall mounted, hidden in a piece of furniture, made fully portable for storage in an out-of-the-way place when not in use, or built as a permanent fixture, occupying a large part of a basement. Regardless of the type of layout you build, it must be held together by some type of rigid structure — the benchwork. The benchwork consists of the sub-roadbed for the track,

the framework, and the mounting brackets or legs.

The framework provides a solid mounting surface for the sub-roadbed and also an anchoring place for scenery. The framework can be a thick sheet of plywood for a small portable layout or it can be a complex network of girders, joists, and legs needed to support a large basement empire.

The sub-roadbed is the wood supporting structure for the track roadbed. For a small model railroad layout using only a sheet of plywood, the plywood serves as both the framework and subroadbed. On larger layouts the subroadbed and the framework are usually two distinct entities.

Sub-roadbed construction methods

Solid top — With this method, the entire layout is built on a sheet of plywood, as shown in fig. 3-3. The solid top has several advantages. First, a minimum of carpentry work is required. Also, the track plan can be drawn full size right on the board and several arrangements can be tried. This method has disadvantages. It is awkward to build track going above the level of the solid top and it is impossible to build track below the solid top. Modifications and repairs are difficult because everything must be done from the top.

Cookie-cutter method — This is an improved modification of the solid-top

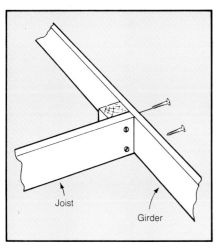

Fig. 3-6. This is butted-grid framework.

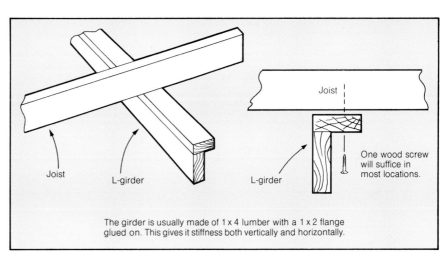

One wood screw will suffice in most locations.

The girder is usually made of 1 x 4 lumber with a 1 x 2 flange glued on. This gives it stiffness both vertically and horizontally.

Fig. 3-8. L-girder framework is strong, lightweight, and adaptable to many situations.

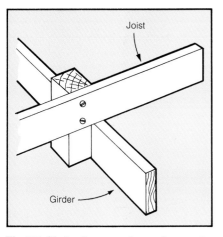

Fig. 3-7. Girder framework requires posts.

method that permits track to be raised or lowered in relation to the surface. The first step in the construction of a cookie-cutter-type layout is similar to the first step in building a solid top. Planning is required so none of the screws or nails used to fasten the solid top to the framing will be situated under any of the track. Once the roadway route is decided, saw cuts are made along both sides of the roadway in those areas where the track is to be raised or lowered. See fig. 3-3. The cutting can be done by hand with a keyhole saw or with a power saber saw. You can lay the track and have it in running order before or after the cutting is done. By using this method, areas can be cut out for a pond, gravel pit, or other type of scenic depression.

Open-top method — With this method, the top of the layout, with the exception of the sub-roadbed, is left open. See fig. 3-3. The sub-roadbed is supported by vertical wood supports (called risers) extending up from the framing. See fig. 3-4. A layout of this type must be planned in three dimensions. We must be concerned not only with the track plan but also with the elevations at each support point along the framing.

Once the risers are cut to the correct height and fastened in place, sub-roadbed may be constructed in several ways. It can be cut from a sheet of plywood the same size as the track plan. This method, which produces *ribbon* sub-roadbed, is fine, but a lot of plywood is wasted. A common sub-roadbed called *lintel* results from cutting and splicing together plywood or other wood strips and fastening them to the risers.

Another sub-roadbed, *spline-lattice* sub-roadbed, features two or three thin edge-mounted wood strips shaped to fit the curves. See fig. 3-5. This sub-roadbed is especially suited for large N scale layouts with sweeping curves of 18″ radius or larger. However, it is difficult to bend the wood strips to form sharper curves. When it can be used, this method is the best because the sub-roadbed is very solid.

Pros and cons

The important advantage of the open-top sub-roadbed method is realism. The track and scenery will be more like that of a real railroad because you're not tied to a flat surface. Also, it is obvious that less wood is required. This can amount to a significant savings on a large layout. On the debit side, this method is more difficult to build than the solid-top or cookie-cutter types.

Actually, all three types of sub-roadbed construction can be effectively combined on larger layouts. The closed-top method is ideal for yard areas. The cookie-cutter technique is a quick and

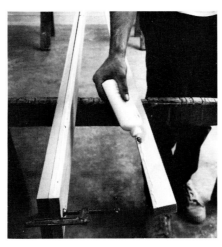

MODEL RAILROADER: A. L. Schmidt.

Fig. 3-9. To construct the L-girders, clamp two 1 x 4's together, drill screw holes through the 1 x 2 into one 1 x 4, and fasten the 1 x 2 to the 1 x 4 with glue and screws.

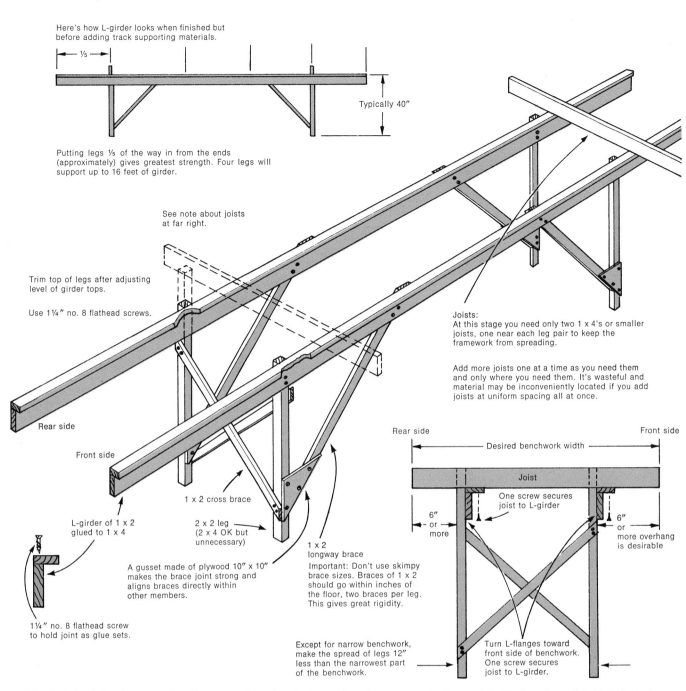

Here's how L-girder looks when finished but before adding track supporting materials.

⅕

Typically 40"

Putting legs ⅕ of the way in from the ends (approximately) gives greatest strength. Four legs will support up to 16 feet of girder.

See note about joists at far right.

Trim top of legs after adjusting level of girder tops.

Use 1¼" no. 8 flathead screws.

Rear side

Front side

Joists:
At this stage you need only two 1 x 4's or smaller joists, one near each leg pair to keep the framework from spreading.

Add more joists one at a time as you need them and only where you need them. It's wasteful and material may be inconveniently located if you add joists at uniform spacing all at once.

L-girder of 1 x 2 glued to 1 x 4

1 x 2 cross brace

2 x 2 leg (2 x 4 OK but unnecessary)

1 x 2 longway brace
Important: Don't use skimpy brace sizes. Braces of 1 x 2 should go within inches of the floor, two braces per leg. This gives great rigidity.

A gusset made of plywood 10" x 10" makes the brace joint strong and aligns braces directly within other members.

1¼" no. 8 flathead screw to hold joint as glue sets.

Rear side

Front side

Desired benchwork width

Joist

One screw secures joist to L-girder

6" or more

6" or more overhang is desirable

Except for narrow benchwork, make the spread of legs 12" less than the narrowest part of the benchwork.

Turn L-flanges toward front side of benchwork. One screw secures joist to L-girder.

Fig. 3-10. L-girder framework relies on engineering design rather than strength of material. The benchwork is light but strong.

easy way to finish relatively level areas. The open-top method lends itself to the more spectacular scenic effects — mountains, lakes, bridges, and trestles.

Framework methods

There are two framing methods commonly used by model railroaders: butted grid and L-girder.

Butted-grid framework — This type of frame consists of girders of 1 x 2 lumber or larger, which run along the edges of the layout area, and crosspieces (called joists) which reach from side to side and across the ends of the area. See fig. 3-6. If the layout is wide, a third girder may be needed down the center.

L-girder framework — The L-girder method of framing appears similar

to the butted-grid method at first glance, but upon closer examination subtle differences become apparent. The significant feature is that the joists rest on top of the girders. See fig. 3-7. The L-girder framing method is popular for model railroad construction. This method derives its name from the shape of the girders, which are inverted Ls. See fig. 3-8. There is an important advantage: all screws that hold the joists to the girders are installed through the foot of the L from the underside. It is easy to remove, add, or relocate a joist at any time during construction or later to make a modification without disturbing anything on the top of the layout.

The placement of table legs for an L-girder frame deserves some special

mention. The most natural place to install table legs is at the corners. However, the best place to locate the legs of an L-girder framework is about one-fifth of the way in from the ends. See fig. 3-10. The legs are sturdier in this position and are not so likely to be kicked.

Which framework method is best?

The butted-grid framework method is ideal for small layouts which use either the solid-top or cookie-cutter sub-roadbed construction. It is quick and easy and results in a solid base for the sub-roadbed.

In my opinion, all layouts larger than 3' x 5' should use the open-top method of sub-roadbed construction and L-girder framework. The combination of

Fig. 3-11. The visual impact of a layout, particularly in a small scale, is greater at eye level than at waist level. Scott Loomer shows the difference 1 foot of elevation can make.

these two methods results in the most versatile construction form. Changes to the layout, even major ones, can be made easily. A large layout represents a substantial investment and it must be adaptable to new ideas and improvements as your modeling skill increases.

Layout height

The layout height is a matter of personal preference. Your layout will look more realistic if you choose a height that places the layout near eye level when you are operating it. See fig. 3-11. Many modelers select a height convenient for working when standing up, and then operate the layout while sitting. If you follow this rule, your layout probably will be 42″ to 48″ above the floor, depending on your height.

Work carefully

Whatever type of benchwork you build, work to the best of your ability. Although you're in a rush to get the first trains rolling, do not rush the benchwork. You may regret it later. Remember, you don't have to be a skilled carpenter to build a solid base for your trackwork. Work slowly and carefully and you'll do all right. The tools necessary for benchwork construction are shown in fig. 3-12.

Power tools can cause serious injury, which is another good reason to take your time and proceed carefully.

Benchwork is the foundation upon which your model railroad rests. Start by building on bedrock.

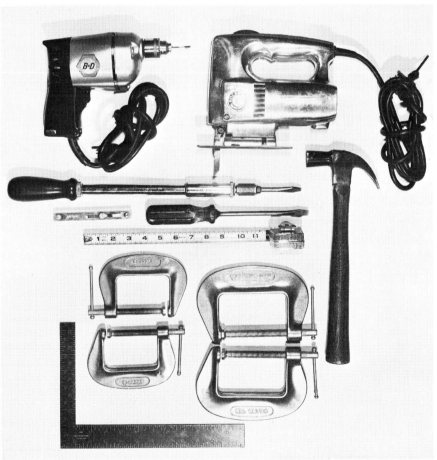

MODEL RAILROADER: A. L. Schmidt.

Fig. 3-12. The construction of your benchwork requires only a few tools: saw, either electric or hand; drill, electric or hand, with a pilot drill; screwdriver (the ratchet type is handy); level; steel tape or folding rule; hammer; square; and several C-clamps.

19

Track – from ballast to golden spike

After the benchwork is completed, we come to a phase of layout construction that has a prototype counterpart — trackwork.

A variety of trackwork supplies is available for N scale. You can duplicate in N scale almost anything that the prototype railroads have done. In addition to employing the many fine commercial products, some advanced N scale modelers are hand laying their own track and achieving even greater realism.

The roadbed

N gauge track can be mounted directly on the wood sub-roadbed. However, using some type of roadbed (or ballast board) material adds to the realism of the layout. The use of roadbed material has several advantages: appearance of the finished trackwork is more realistic, track installation is easier, and train noise is deadened. See fig. 4-1.

The terms *roadbed* and *ballast* have slightly different meanings in model railroading than they do in real railroading. In railroad terminology, the roadbed is the graded earth upon which the crushed stone, gravel, or cinder ballast is applied. See fig. 4-2. The ties are set in the ballast and the track is spiked to the ties. Prototype ballast serves two main purposes: It supports the ties and distributes the traffic load over the roadbed. It also helps drain water from the ties and thus extends their life.

Specifications for ballast vary greatly from railroad to railroad. Generally, broken stone with diameters between ¾″ and 2½″ is used for ballasting mainline track. Cinders frequently are used for ballasting yard tracks. A ballast depth of 8″ to 12″ is common. The ballast of newly laid track is level with the top of the ties.

For our model railroad work we simulate the appearance of real trackwork without using identical trackwork installation methods. Our scale track is fastened to a strip of roadbed material. Ballast then is applied between the ties and over the beveled edges of the roadbed strip. (Some modelers prefer to call this strip of material the ballast board. Use whichever term you prefer.)

Many materials can be used for the roadbed strip. The two most popular materials for N scale roadbeds are Homasote and cork.

Homasote is a type of wallboard sold through lumberyards. It makes a fine roadbed material. It takes spikes or nails well, deadens train noise effectively, and doesn't warp out of shape when plaster scenery is added. It also has disadvantages. It may be difficult to obtain because many lumberyards do not stock it, although many will order it for you. It comes in 4 x 8-foot sheets, much larger than many modelers need for their N scale layout. It must be cut to fit the track plan and if you want to simulate the prototype, the edges of the Homasote strips must be beveled as shown in fig. 4-2. Cutting and beveling Homasote is a messy job. Wear a dust mask when performing these jobs.

Cork, in my opinion, is the best roadbed material for N scale. It has all the advantages of Homasote and none of the disadvantages. Cork roadbed strips are sold in most hobby shops. It comes in strips which have one beveled edge and one square-cut edge. See fig. 4-3. To form a single-track roadbed, two strips of cork are laid side by side with the square edges butted together and the beveled edges to the outside. Wider roadbeds can be made by mating the beveled edges together. Cork roadbed also is laterally flexible so it can be easily shaped to fit the track plan.

The route the roadbed is to follow must be carefully laid out. If you are using sectional track, take extra time to temporarily install the track on the sub-roadbed to ensure that the track fits the plan before you permanently install the roadbed.

Homasote board must be cut to fit the contours of the plan and also to the correct width. If you are modeling a well-kept main line, the edges of the Homasote should be beveled to conform to the roadbed profile shown in fig. 4-2.

As previously mentioned, cork roadbed strips are laterally flexible and they can be shaped to fit the track plan.

Homasote and cork roadbed can be fastened to the sub-roadbed using small nails and white glue. Homasote can be fastened using glue alone. Cork roadbed requires a number of ½″ wire nails to hold it in the correct position until the glue dries. Place weights on the roadbed and allow the glue to dry overnight.

The track

There are two approaches to N scale trackwork. First, you can hand lay your track in much the same manner as the prototype railroads do. This method is common in the larger modeling scales. Individual ties are laid on the roadbed and then the rail is spiked to the ties. Second, you may use prefabricated track sections (the majority of N scale modelers do). The techniques required to hand lay track are reviewed from time to time in MODEL RAILROADER Magazine.

Sectional and flexible track — Train sets usually include pieces of track which form an oval or other simple track plan when joined together. This

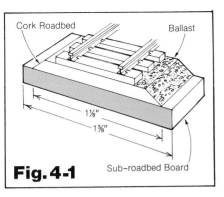

Fig. 4-1

Bill Neustedter.

Fig. 4-3. Cork roadbed comes in two strips that must be split apart before laying.

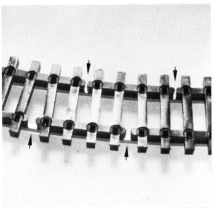

MODEL RAILROADER: A. L. Schmidt.

Fig. 4-5. Gaps in the tie strip of flexible track allow the track to be curved to fit any track plan.

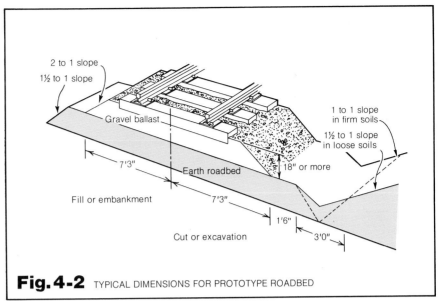

Fig. 4-2 TYPICAL DIMENSIONS FOR PROTOTYPE ROADBED

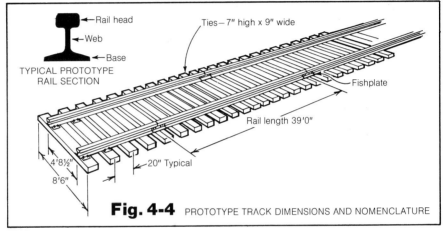

Fig. 4-4 PROTOTYPE TRACK DIMENSIONS AND NOMENCLATURE

type of track is called sectional track. Each manufacturer of N scale sectional track, such as Atlas and Peco, offers different lengths of straight track, different radii of curves, and different types of switches.

Sectional track is easiest to work with and therefore is ideal for beginners. The advantage of sectional track is that it can be assembled without any cutting or other handwork. A disadvantage of sectional track is that track plans must be designed around fixed-radius curves. However, there are many track configurations possible with sectional track. (Another Kalmbach book edited by Russ Larson — *N Scale Model Railroad Track Plans* — contains 65 plans using sectional track.)

Flexible track is a special type of sectional track. Although manufacturers offer slightly different lengths, all sec-

tions are about 3 feet long. This track easily can be formed into any type of curve. There are spaces in the plastic supporting strips under the rails that make the track flexible. See fig. 4-5. Using flexible track you can achieve a more realistic layout because you are not tied to fixed-radius curves.

A disadvantage of flexible track, for the beginner, is that some rail cutting is required. When a section of flexible track is curved, the rail ends come out uneven and the longer one must be cut back. Three-foot lengths occasionally will have to be cut into shorter pieces for particular trackwork.

Interchangeability — There are two different methods used to join N scale track sections together. The usual method uses rail joiners (fishplates) opposite each other, while one brand, Arnold Rapido, uses staggered rail joiners. See fig. 4-6. If necessary, the two types of track can be joined together. Arnold Rapido offers a special track section and special rail joiners for this purpose.

Switches and curve radii — Two factors greatly affect layout operation: 1.) The radius of the curves. 2.) The radius (also referred to as "number") of the

switches (more properly called turnouts) that are used. If the curves are very sharp, say 7″, long wheelbase equipment will bind in the curve as shown in fig. 4-7. Even if the equipment successfully negotiates the curve, the added drag on the locomotive may result in jerky operation. Although the operational consideration is the most important, the appearance also must be considered. The excessive overhang of long wheelbase equipment rolling around sharp curves gives the operation a toylike appearance.

Two types of switches are offered in N scale: fixed-radius switches and numbered switches. The differences are illustrated in fig. 4-8. The numbered switches are more prototypical; however, the fixed-radius type have track planning advantages if using sectional track: The radii employed for the switches match those offered for the curved sections.

As a guide, plan your layout with the largest radius curves and the highest number (largest radius) switches possible in the space available. Figure 2-10 in Chapter 2 offers guidelines for planning, including the selection of curve radii.

Fig. 4-6. Rapido track has staggered joints; other brands, opposed joints.

Fig. 4-7. Long passenger cars operate poorly and look unrealistic on sharp curves.

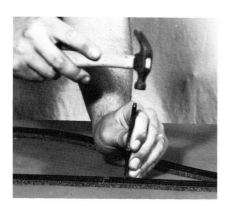

Fig. 4-9. A light hammer and a nail set are the best tracklaying tools.

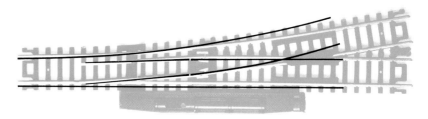

Fig. 4-8. Fixed-radius switches (black lines) require less space, but numbered switches (photograph) with straight track through the frog are more realistic.

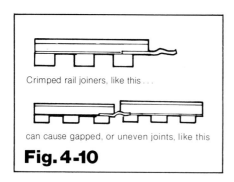

Crimped rail joiners, like this . . .

can cause gapped, or uneven joints, like this

Fig. 4-10

Fig. 4-11. A yardstick with holes, a pencil, and a thumbtack make a good compass.

Tracklaying tips

The most common technique of fastening the track to the roadbed is to drive small wire nails (½" No. 18s often are used) through holes in the center of the plastic tie strip as shown in fig. 4-9. N gauge track is usually sold with predrilled holes. If your brand of track does not have predrilled mounting holes, you can drill your own by using a pin vise and a No. 60 drill.

Do not tap or press the nails down completely to tie-top level. A little play will allow the track to "float." This prevents the possibility of the plastic tie strip springing away from the rail, and also makes it easier to remove the track at a later date if necessary.

Do not kink the rail joiners when you join track sections together. A kinked rail joiner prevents the tracks from aligning vertically as shown in fig. 4-10.

Leave a very small gap between track pieces at 2- to 3-foot intervals to allow for expansion of the track or contraction of the roadbed owing to changes in temperature.

When laying flexible track, make sure that the curves are smooth by maintaining the same radius from beginning to end. A cardstock template cut to correct radius for the inside edge of the track is of great help. Another effective way to obtain smooth curves is to plot them on the sub-roadbed using a yardstick as a large compass as shown in fig. 4-11.

When flexible track is curved, the outside rail becomes shorter than the inside rail. The excess length of the inner rail must be trimmed to square off the rail ends. Use a rail nipper (fig. 4-12) for this rail, cutting and then filing the rail ends smooth (fig. 4-13). In order to accommodate the rail joiners, a slot must be cut horizontally along the top of the first ties as shown in figs. 4-14 and 4-15. An alternate method of providing room for the rail joiners is simply to cut off the end ties. After the track sections are joined together, slip cutdown ties back in place under the joiners. The bonded ballast will hold them in place.

Check the track gauge frequently when laying track. Track is most likely to slip out of gauge at the points where two sections of flexible track are joined, especially if the joint occurs on a curve. Several track gauges are available. The Kadee track gauge is shown being used in fig. 4-16.

Installing track switches isn't difficult, but the serious operational prob-

Fig. 4-12. Cut the track to length using rail nippers.

Fig. 4-15. Slip the rail joiner over the base of the rail.

Fig. 4-13. Square the rail ends using a flat file.

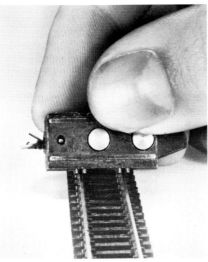

Fig. 4-16. A gauge, such as Kadee's, helps you check track alignment.

Fig. 4-14. Slice away the simulated spikes with a razor blade, knife, or saw.

lems occur at the switches if they are not properly installed. Here are some tips on how to avoid most of these problems.

Make certain that switchpoints move freely after installation. Use only a few brads to hold the switch to the roadbed. This will allow it to "float" a little and the chances of binding are reduced. Any binding may stop the switchpoints from contacting the stock rails.

When spreading ballast, be careful not to foul the switchpoints. The smallest piece of ballast lodged between the points and the stock rails may interfere with operation. If it is your first layout, omit ballast entirely from the frog to the switchpoints.

Make sure that the sharp ends of the switchpoints rest tightly against the stock rails so that the wheel flanges will not ride between the rails and the points. You may have to file the points sharper to prevent the wheels from "picking the points" and derailing.

Ballasting the track

Many brands of N scale ballast are available at most hobby shops. N scale ballast is either fine sand or crushed limestone which has been graded for uniformity and colored. The difference in realism between un-ballasted and ballasted track is quite dramatic.

Track ballasting can be done either before or after the scenery is added to the layout. There are several methods for fixing the ballast to the roadbed and ties. The method I'm going to explain, and the one I prefer, is the bonded ballast method.

The first step in this method is to apply ballast between the rails. A paper cup or a teaspoon can be used to do this. Use your finger or a small brush to evenly distribute the ballast along the track.

Next, build a shoulder of ballast on the outside of the rails. Make the shoulder even or irregular depending on the kind of railroad you are modeling. One way to form an even shoulder is to hold a strip of wood or cardstock on edge about 2 scale feet from the tie ends and then fill the space from the

rail to the strip with ballast. When you slide the strip away, the ballast will fall into a nice even slope.

Next the ballast must be fixed in place without disturbing its natural look. The bonded ballast method will accomplish this. Two commonly used bonding agents are white glue and acrylic polymer medium. The application procedure is the same with both bonding agents.

If you are using a white glue for the bonding agent, prepare a solution of 1 part glue and 4 parts water. If you're using acrylic polymer medium, prepare a solution of 1 part medium to 1 part water. Acrylic polymer medium may be purchased at art supply stores.

Next, mix a solution of water and liquid detergent in the ratio of one capful of detergent per quart of water. This is the wetting agent. Fill a window-cleaner sprayer with wetting agent and spray a mist of this mixture over about 2 feet of the ballasted track. Be careful to spray gently so as not to disturb the ballast.

Using an eyedropper, carefully place a few drops of the bonding agent between the ties and also outside the rails at regular intervals perhaps every four to six ties. The bonding agent will permeate the ballast because of the detergent in the wetting agent. Continue to apply drops of bonding agent to the ballast until all the wetted ballast has been impregnated by the bonding agent.

Spray the wetting agent on another 2 feet or so of ballast and follow with application of the bonding agent. Continue the procedure until all the ballast is fixed.

The bonding agent will dry overnight. It will hold the ballast in place but the ballast will still look natural — as it did when first applied.

Many newcomers to model railroading believe that special skill and knowledge are needed to wire a layout. This is not so. A layout can be wired correctly by following step-by-step instructions. However, as with most projects, it helps to have a basic knowledge of the subject. In the space of this one chapter I'm going to present some basic information on wiring which I hope will help you tackle this phase of your layout construction with confidence. If you find this facet of the hobby interesting, I suggest you read the book *How to Wire Your Model Railroad* by Linn Westcott.

ABC's of electricity

Before you can understand the principles of train control and wiring, you have to know a little bit about electricity. If you look at electricity as a form of energy, you are on the way to understanding it. Electricity is a form of energy. It has the capacity to do work.

Electrical energy, like all forms of energy, must be measured if it is to be understood and used. The units of measurement for electrical energy are volts, amperes, and watts.

Electric current is the movement or flow of electrons. The unit of measure is the ampere.

Electromotive force is the pressure that causes the electrons to move. The unit of measure is the volt.

Electric power is the work the electric current is doing. The unit of measure is the watt. For the d.c. (direct current) circuits we use, power is the product of current and electromotive force — watts equals amperes times volts. Your electric bill states the power your home has used for the month in watt-hours or kilowatt-hours. A watt-hour is a unit of work equal to the power of one watt operating for one hour. A kilowatt-hour is 1000 watt-hours.

Resistance is the difficulty with which electric current passes through a substance. Copper and silver have low resistances — current passes through them easily. Rubber has a high resistance; in fact, it passes so little current that it makes a good insulator. The unit of resistance is the ohm. One volt of pressure can force 1 ampere of current through 1 ohm of resistance. Twice as much pressure should force twice as much current through the resistance: 2 volts can force 2 amperes of current through 1 ohm of resistance. Note, by the way, that since power is the product of current and voltage, the power is now four times as great: 4 watts.

What if the resistance changes? For a given voltage, the current flow increases if the resistance is lowered, and it decreases if the resistance is raised. The current flow in a circuit is arithmetically equal to the voltage divided by the resistance. The fundamental relationship of electrical units is Ohm's Law. It is often expressed as the formula $I = E/R$, where I is the current, E is the voltage, and R is the resistance.

N scale locomotive motors

The motors in N scale model locomotives are the permanent-magnet type, designed to operate at top speed on 12 volts d.c. Understanding how the motor works helps you understand the fine points of controlling the motor.

You've probably played with magnets, and you know that one magnet brought closer to another can make the second one turn around and snap over to the first. Each magnet has two ends or poles, termed north and south corresponding to the earth's magnetic field. Like poles of two magnets repel each other, and unlike poles attract. Thus if you bring the south pole of a

magnet near the south end of a compass needle, the needle will swing away and the north end will come around to the magnet in your hand. That, basically, is the principle of the motor. The compass needle motor works for half a revolution but something is needed to bring the needle around again.

What if you could change the polarity of the compass needle? Current

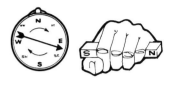

flowing through a wire creates a magnetic field around the wire. Forming the wire into a coil like a spring intensifies the field, and a piece of iron in the center of the coil serves as a kind of focus for the magnetic field. When current flows through the coil, the piece of iron becomes a magnet, with a north

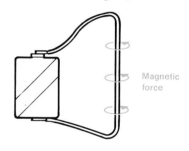

pole at one end and a south pole at the other. If you change the direction of the current — run it through the coil backwards — the polarity of the magnetic field reverses.

Let's replace the compass needle with the coil and the piece of iron

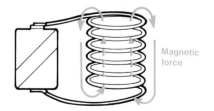

mounted so that they can rotate just as the compass needle does. In the place of the magnet we have been holding in our hand, let's install a horseshoe-shaped permanent magnet to straddle the ends of the coil and the piece of iron. To supply current to the coil, we will use a flashlight battery. Current passing from the battery to one end of the coil and returning to the battery from the other end of the coil will cre-

viring

ate a magnetic field in the coil and the iron, and the assembly will turn on its axis as it is attracted by the appropriate pole of the permanent magnet.

To keep the coil turning, we have to

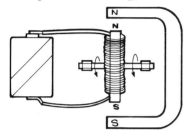

reverse the current in the coil so that each end of the coil becomes attracted to the opposite pole of the magnet. One way to do this would be to disconnect each end of the coil where it joins the battery and connect the ends to the opposite terminals of the battery. Naturally, this would be slow and impractical. We need a switch that reverses the polarity of the coil.

For a switch, let's use a drum-shaped piece of metal split into halves. Our coil is turning on an axis or shaft. We install the two halves over the shaft much as you would clamp your hands around a large vase. Now the drum halves, shaft, and coil are all part of the same rotating assembly. Each end of the coil is connected to one of the drum halves. The battery, instead of being connected to the coil, is connected by wires to two contacts, called brushes, which are placed in a fixed, non-rotating position against the two drum halves.

Current passes from the battery to the brush to the drum half. From there it passes through the coil, creating a magnetic field, and the assembly rotates to the pull of the permanent mag-

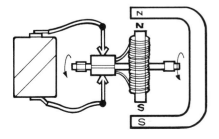

net. In rotating, the drum halves come in contact with the opposite brushes. Current passes through the coil again, but in the opposite direction! The polarity has been reversed, and the assembly rotates again — in the same direction — to the pull of the magnet. We have a motor!

By attaching the shaft to gears, we are on our way to having useful work produced .

Now for a few terms:

Field — the permanent magnet around the outside.

Armature — the rotating part of the motor.

Commutator — the drum-shaped part of the armature that routes the current to the coils in the proper direction.

Armature core pole — the iron part of the armature with the wire wound around it. Model motors usually have three or five armature core poles.

Brushes — the two pieces of graphite that rub on the commutator and carry current to it. One brush normally has a wire attached to it for bringing current from the tender or one truck; the other brush usually is grounded to the frame of the locomotive.

Train control

Train-control units, commonly called power packs or throttles, come in assorted sizes, shapes, colors, and degrees of quality.

The circuit shown in fig. 5-2 provides a simple, practical method of controlling model locomotive speed. The battery converts chemical energy to electrical energy and the rheostat converts some of the electrical energy to heat. The rheostat is a variable resistor that controls the voltage to the motor, and thus the speed of the motor, by wasting some of the voltage to produce heat. The chief disadvantage of this circuit, common in the early days of the hobby, is that the battery must be recharged after each operating session.

All photos, unless otherwise credited, MODEL RAILROADER: A. L. Schmidt.

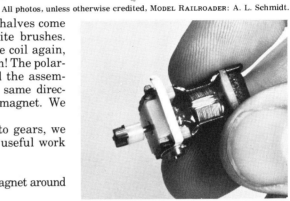

Fig. 5-1. Tiny permanent-magnet motors such as this power N scale locomotives.

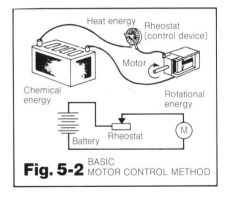

Fig. 5-2 BASIC MOTOR CONTROL METHOD

Fig. 5-3. Before transistor throttles, rheostats were used for speed control.

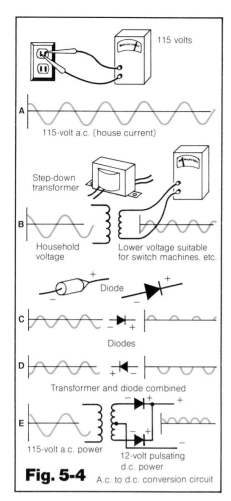

Fig. 5-4 A.c. to d.c. conversion circuit

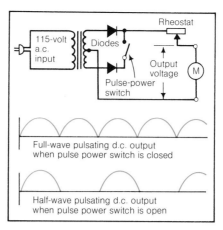

Fig. 5-6. The pulse-power switch is an important feature of a power pack.

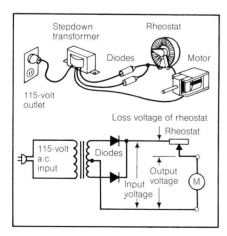

Fig. 5-5. Basic power pack components, both pictorial and schematic.

For practicality, the battery of fig. 5-2 must be replaced with a device that can convert 115-volt a.c. house current to 12-volt d.c. Fig. 5-4 shows a stepdown transformer, which reduces the voltage and also completely isolates the tracks and locomotives from the house current, and a pair of diodes, or rectifiers, that allow the current to flow in only one direction. (A permanent-magnet motor connected to alternating current would try to reverse its rotation 120 times a second. It would have an active but short life.) Adding the rheostat as in

fig. 5-5 we have what is commonly called a power pack. It is the most widely used type of train control. It is rugged and economical.

The rheostat is the one part of the power pack that performs less than ideally. Instead of controlling the voltage to the motor directly, the rheostat wastes an amount of voltage depending on the load the motor is pulling. Take an example: A particular engine with its train starts at 3.5 volts. Before the wheels turn it draws .16 ampere, and after the wheels begin to move it draws .11 ampere. Before the engine moves the rheostat wastes about 8.5 volts, but at the same setting after the engine starts to move it drops only 5.5 volts because of the decrease in motor current. The motor voltage increases suddenly from 3.5 volts to 6.5 volts, and the train leaps ahead.

Among the ways of combating the jackrabbit start are pulsed power, a gentle hand on the throttle, a variable transfomer to replace the rheostat, and a transistor throttle.

Power packs vary in quality. Some that are sold for a bottom price may have mechanical parts that don't stand up and electrical parts too skimpy for the load, unable, for example, to handle

doubleheaded trains or trains with lighted passenger cars. A well-established make such as Model Rectifier's MRC line can deliver the claimed ratings.

Features to look for when selecting a power pack are adequate power rating, taper-wound rheostat, overload protection, and pulse-power switch.

The power pack you select must be able to power all the locomotives needed to pull your longest train and in addition must light the train's lights. Therefore a more powerful pack is needed to operate a long lighted passenger train with three powered diesel units at the head end than to operate a four-car way freight behind a single locomotive.

As a general rule, the power pack should be able to deliver .2 ampere for each locomotive to be operated simultaneously plus .05 ampere for each grain-of-wheat lamp. The .2-ampere rating for the motor is only an average. To determine the current required for each locomotive, you must measure the current drawn by each when running at full load at 12 volts.

A common rating for an N scale power pack is 1 ampere at 12 volts (12 watts). This rating is adequate for most individual layouts. The long trains op-

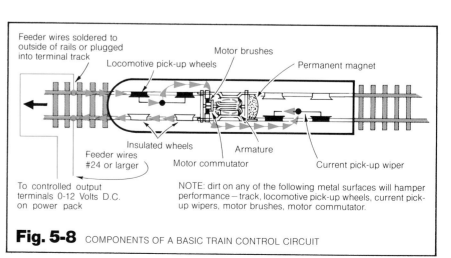

Fig. 5-8 COMPONENTS OF A BASIC TRAIN CONTROL CIRCUIT

Fig. 5-7. Basic transistor control, both pictorial and schematic.

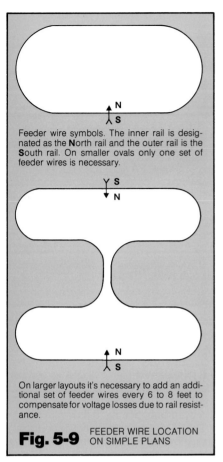

Feeder wire symbols. The inner rail is designated as the **N**orth rail and the outer rail is the **S**outh rail. On smaller ovals only one set of feeder wires is necessary.

On larger layouts it's necessary to add an additional set of feeder wires every 6 to 8 feet to compensate for voltage losses due to rail resistance.

Fig. 5-9 FEEDER WIRE LOCATION ON SIMPLE PLANS

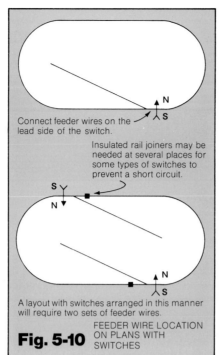

Connect feeder wires on the lead side of the switch.

Insulated rail joiners may be needed at several places for some types of switches to prevent a short circuit.

A layout with switches arranged in this manner will require two sets of feeder wires.

Fig. 5-10 FEEDER WIRE LOCATION ON PLANS WITH SWITCHES

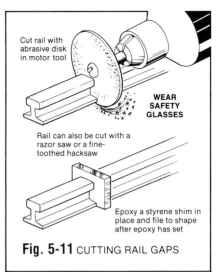

Cut rail with abrasive disk in motor tool

WEAR SAFETY GLASSES

Rail can also be cut with a razor saw or a fine-toothed hacksaw

Epoxy a styrene shim in place and file to shape after epoxy has set

Fig. 5-11 CUTTING RAIL GAPS

erated by clubs require a higher power rating.

A taper-wound rheostat is designed so the resistance change per degree of control-knob rotation is greater at low voltage than it is at higher-speed settings, spreading the speed control through the entire rotation of the knob.

The pulse-power switch cuts out one of the diodes, making the circuit a half-wave rectifier rather than a full-wave rectifier. See fig. 5-6. The rough, pul-

sating d.c. that the half-wave rectifier provides results in smoother starting for the same reason that it is easier to drive a nail with many small blows of a hammer than with a single heavy push. Half-wave d.c. has one disadvantage. It causes the motor to run warmer. The pulse-power switch lets you use pulse power for starting and full-wave power for over-the-road runs.

A resettable circuit breaker is the best overload protection for a power pack. If the load exceeds the current rating of the pack, the circuit breaker trips, turning the power off. This protects the pack and also may protect the equipment causing the overload or short circuit.

Two features you may find in the more expensive power packs are vari-

able-transformer control and transistor throttles. The variable transformer resembles a rheostat. Both devices have a sliding wiper running over turns of wire. However, they are completely different electrically. The variable transformer has low-resistance wire, and the voltage difference across the windings is barely affected by the load current. The wiper of the variable transformer selects the portion of the household voltage to be applied to the input side of the step-down transformer.

The advantages of the variable transformer are due to the fact that no resistance is added to the circuit to control the speed of the locomotive. Voltage to the track is controlled directly and is thus unaffected by the load on the motor. In addition, less heat is generated inside the power pack than is generated with a rheostat.

Transistor throttles also control voltage directly, and the very low voltages and currents in transistor circuits allow exotic features to be added to the control circuit for simulating momen-

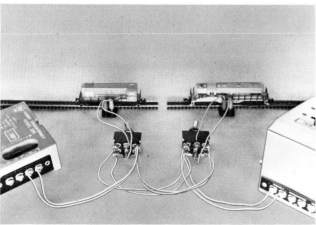

MODEL RAILROADER: Russ Larson.

Fig. 5-12. Here are two blocks shown wired for dual cab control. The gap between the blocks is exaggerated for clarity.

Fig. 5-13. Mounting the dp.dt. toggles of fig. 5-12 on a control panel completes the dual cab control system.

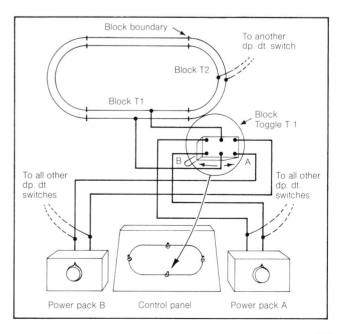

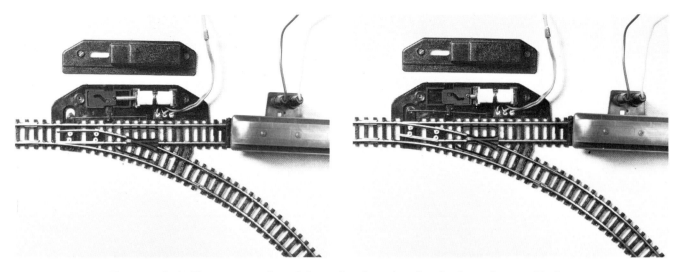

Fig. 5-14. (Left) The armature faces left, setting the points for the through route. Facing right (right), the armature sets the points for the diverging route.

tum, separating throttle and brake actions (with separate control knobs), and improving the response of motors both when starting and when changing loads. The number of these features you get in a transistor throttle depends on the price you pay.

A discussion of the electronics of the transistor throttle is beyond the scope of this chapter. Articles on the subject appear from time to time in MODEL RAILROADER Magazine. Several transistor throttles suitable for operating N scale trains are available — check at your local hobby shop.

Safety

The low-voltage electricity used to operate N scale trains is not dangerous. You will not receive a serious shock by touching the output terminals of a power pack. However, power packs operate on 115-volt a.c. house current, which is dangerous. This 115-volt a.c. is present at the input terminals of the transformer inside the power pack case. For this reason, opening the power pack case and attempting repairs yourself is dangerous. Make sure you always turn the power pack off or unplug it when it is not in use.

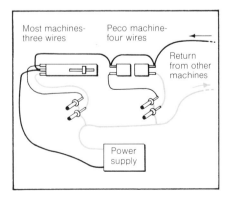

Fig. 5-15. A wiring diagram for employing pushbuttons, such as Browa (Walthers) or Radio Shack, to control switch machines.

Wiring for one-train operation

One-train wiring is simple. Run two wires from the controlled d.c. terminals of your power pack to the track as shown in fig. 5-8. Most hobby shops sell suitable wire. Each brand of N scale track has a track clip or terminal section for making the connections to the track. The only disadvantage of these terminal track sections is that they are conspicuous. Connections to the track can be almost unnoticeable if you route the feeder wires under the layout, bring them up alongside the track, and solder them to the outside of the rail.

On small oval tracks connect the two wires to the track anywhere on the layout. Larger ovals require an additional pair of feeder wires at the opposite side of the layout. See fig. 5-9. These additional wires are used because the rail has resistance, and over many feet of length this rail resistance coupled with the resistance of the rail joiners may cause a noticeable voltage drop. This voltage drop causes changes in train speed as the train travels around a layout with only one pair of feeders.

Track plans with turnouts require more thought. Most brands of N scale turnouts are wired internally so that both routes through the turnout are powered regardless of the position of the points of the turnout. Other brands, such as Peco, are of the power-routing type. The switch points route the electrical power as well as the train. Layouts with this type of turnout must be wired with the feeder wires at the point end of the switch. See fig. 5-10.

Wiring for two-train operation

Two or more trains can be operated simultaneously under independent control on your layout. The best way to accomplish this is through "dual cab control." To wire a layout for dual cab control you must divide it into electrically insulated sections called "blocks."

Most good track plans show suggested block boundaries. They are indicated by slash marks as shown in fig. 5-13. You can either install plastic insulated rail joiners at these locations as you lay the track, or you can cut gaps at these points with a razor saw after the track has been laid. See fig. 5-11.

Two locomotives are shown being operated by cab control in fig. 5-12. I have exaggerated the gap between the blocks for clarity. Notice that each block of track is wired to the center terminals of a double-pole, double-throw (dp.dt) center-off toggle switch. The right-hand terminals of each toggle are connected to the power pack on the left side, and the left-hand terminals are connected to the pack on the right. Thus when the toggle is flipped in the direction of either power pack, that pack is connected to the block controlled by that toggle switch. When the switch is in the center (off) position, neither pack is connected to the block.

That is all dual cab control is, except that the toggle switches must be mounted on a control panel, which can be placed between the two power packs for accessibility.

Operating a dual cab control system is easy. You flip the toggles that control the blocks along the route of your train toward your throttle as your train travels around the layout. As your train leaves a block, return the switch for that block to the off position so that the other "engineer" knows that the block is now unoccupied.

Switch-machine control

Track switches or turnouts can be thrown by hand or operated electrically. The electrical devices used to operate turnouts are called switch machines. They are twin-coil solenoids that move a metal slug called the armature (not to be confused with the armature mentioned in our description of the motor) back and forth, fig. 5-14,

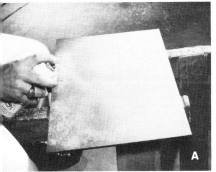
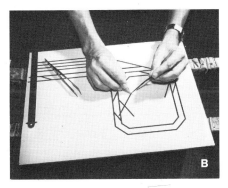

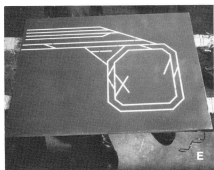
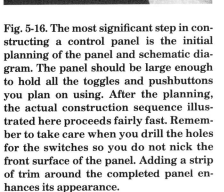
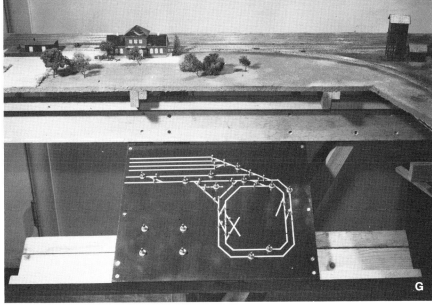

Fig. 5-16. The most significant step in constructing a control panel is the initial planning of the panel and schematic diagram. The panel should be large enough to hold all the toggles and pushbuttons you plan on using. After the planning, the actual construction sequence illustrated here proceeds fairly fast. Remember to take care when you drill the holes for the switches so you do not nick the front surface of the panel. Adding a strip of trim around the completed panel enhances its appearance.

and the motion of the armature moves the points of the turnout.

Switch machines operate on either a.c. or d.c. of approximately 16 volts. They draw an instantaneous current of between .5 and 1.5 amperes. They need only a momentary spurt of electricity, or they will burn out. Special controllers and pushbuttons are available for switch machines. Some brands of turnouts are packaged with a controller.

Generally the switch machines are powered from the a.c. accessory terminals of the power pack. Leads run from these terminals to the switch-machine controller or pushbutton and from there to the switch machine.

The controllers manufactured by Atlas and Bachmann plug together so you need run wires from the power pack only to the first controller. Three leads must run from the controller to the switch machine. Pushbuttons, available at electronic stores, also work well for controlling switch machines. Two pushbuttons are needed for each machine, one for each position of the turnout, wired as in fig. 5-15.

The high instantaneous current drawn by the switch machines can interfere with train operation if both the switch machines and the train are powered from the same power pack. The train may slow down or stop when a switch is thrown. It is best to operate your switch machines from a separate power pack. You may not be able to invest in one right away, but it is something to consider for the future.

Control panels

If you decide to wire your layout for two-train operation and you use electric switch machines, you will want a control panel that includes both the block toggles and the turnout controls. There are many types of control panels. One type that works well for most model railroaders entails mounting all the block control switches on a panel which carries a schematic diagram of

the track plan. This method makes operation easier because you can see at a glance which block is controlled by each switch. Pushbuttons for switch-machine control can be inserted in the schematic at the point corresponding to the turnout they control.

Most suppliers of N gauge track offer electrically operated uncoupling ramps. If you decide to use electric uncouplers, you will want to put their controls in the panel also. Couplers are discussed in Chapter 8.

Start construction of the panel by laying out a schematic diagram of your track plan on a piece of paper. Make it large enough to accommodate all the toggles and pushbuttons you intend to place in it.

Cut a piece of tempered Masonite

Fig. 5-17. A neat control panel cabling job like this one by Walt Olsen helps take the strain off the connections and makes the panel easier to troubleshoot.

Walt Olsen.

WIRE-NUT SPLICE

Join wires with a few loose twists. Screwing internally threaded nut onto wires twists them securely together.

RATTAIL SPLICE   **TEE SPLICE**

Twist wires together, solder, clip off ends, tape joint. Twist wires together, solder, trim end, tape joint.

SOLDER TERMINALS

Crimp wire, solder, trim end.

Wrong   Right
SCREW TERMINALS

Fig. 5-18 ELECTRICAL WIRE CONNECTION METHODS

large enough for the schematic to fit on it. Paint the Masonite white or some light color, fig. 5-16a.

When the paint is thoroughly dry, lay out the schematic on the panel with ⅛"-wide masking tape, fig. 5-16b. Spray the panel with dark-color paint, fig. 5-16c. When this paint is thoroughly dry, peel off the masking tape, figs. 5-16d and 5-16e.

Drill holes for the toggles (¹⁵/₃₂") and pushbuttons, and mount them on the panel. Wire the panel. It is easier to wire it now than after you mount it to the layout. Run the leads from the switches and pushbuttons to one side of a terminal strip. Later you can wire the track and switch machines to the other side of the terminal strip.

Mount the panel on a simple 1" x 1" or 1" x 2" frame and fasten the assembly to the benchwork.

Lamp wiring

Lights add realism to a layout. You will want lights in buildings and streetlights. These lamps can be powered by either a.c. or d.c. You should operate the lamps at somewhat less than their rated voltage to extend their life. If you plan to have many lights on your layout, it is a good idea to operate them from a separate power supply.

Wiring tips

Wiring a layout properly requires more than merely connecting wires between the proper points. Routing the wires under the layout and their identification are as important as the electrical connections themselves. Electrical problems are easier to locate on a properly wired layout.

The first step is to label all the block toggle switches and switch-machine controls. Commonly used designations are T1, T2, T3, etc., for block **T**oggles and W1, W2, etc., for s**W**itch machine controls. Either label each switch at the back of the control panel or note their designations on a sketch of the panel. Assign a number or letter to each terminal of each switch. As you wire the layout, label each end of each wire with its switch designation and terminal identification. The easiest way to tag wires is with a piece of masking tape looped around the wire and folded

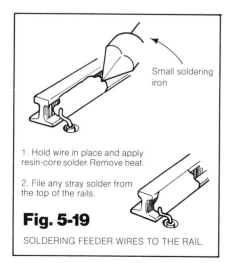

1. Hold wire in place and apply resin-core solder. Remove heat.

2. File any stray solder from the top of the rails.

Fig. 5-19

SOLDERING FEEDER WIRES TO THE RAIL

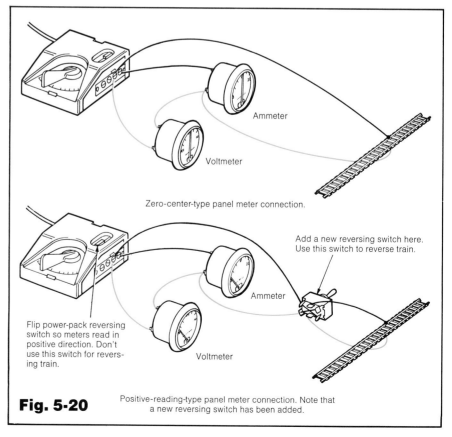

Zero-center-type panel meter connection.

Flip power-pack reversing switch so meters read in positive direction. Don't use this switch for reversing train.

Add a new reversing switch here. Use this switch to reverse train.

Fig. 5-20

Positive-reading-type panel meter connection. Note that a new reversing switch has been added.

Fig. 5-21. A multimeter such as this is a handy piece of test equipment to have when an electrical problem arises.

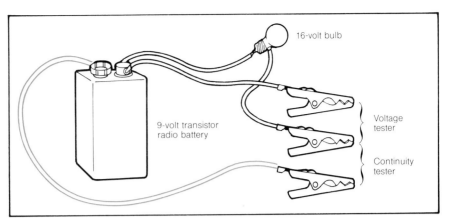

Fig. 5-22. If you don't want to buy a multimeter, you can build an inexpensive voltage indicator/continuity checker such as this one. Caution: Use it only for low voltage.

back on itself. It is also handy to use different colored wires for different purposes; for example, black and white for track feeders, yellow for lamps, red and green for the two coils of the switch machines, blue for uncouplers, and brown for the common return.

The layout wiring should be as inconspicuous as possible. Route all the wires under the layout and up through holes drilled next to the connection point.

The wires do not need to be grouped into cables, but the cables are neater and less prone to damage. Figure 5-17 shows the cabling job done on a control panel built by Walt Olsen.

Don't take the most direct route with the wires. You will create a rat's nest. Take a circuitous route, allow more wire length than you think is necessary, and take your time.

Good electrical connections are important. They must be sound, both mechanically and electrically. When connecting wires, do not rely on the solder alone to hold the wire to its terminal. Crimp the lead around the terminal to ensure good mechanical connection, and then solder the joint, fig. 5-18.

To solder feeder wire to a rail, drill a hole through the roadbed just outside the base of the rail. Thread the feeder wire up through the hole, hold it in place temporarily with a couple of straight pins, and solder it to the rail, fig. 5-19. Use resin-core solder (acid flux will corrode the rail) and a hot soldering iron. Apply the heat and make the joint quickly to avoid melting the ties. It takes practice to get the hang of this operation, so practice on a scrap piece of track before trying it on the layout.

Electrical test equipment

Locating the source of an electrical problem on a model railroad can be a frustrating trial-and-error process unless you know how to make some basic electrical measurements. To do it you need test equipment: voltmeter, ammeter, and ohmmeter.

Voltage always is measured across a resistance. The voltmeter must be in parallel with the item across which the voltage is being measured. The most common voltage measurements on a layout are the d.c. voltages: across the power pack's controlled-d.c. terminals, across the rails, and across the locomotive motor.

To measure current you must insert an ammeter in series with the circuit so that the current flows through the meter.

Many modelers include both a voltmeter and an ammeter in the control panel for each power pack or cab. A voltmeter that reads from 0 to 20 volts d.c. is ideal. The ammeter should have a range of from 0 to 1 ampere d.c. Two types of panel maters are common: positive-reading and zero-center. The zero-center type is easier to install and indicates both magnitude and polarity of the output voltage and current.

A portable voltmeter and an ohmmeter are helpful for troubleshooting. The panel-mounted voltmeter indicates the voltage at the power pack. The portable meter can measure the voltage at various points along the track and at the locomotive. An ohmmeter is handy for checking the continuity of circuits.

You can buy a volt-ohmmeter that can be used for both measurements. A multimeter, fig. 5-21, can measure voltage, current, and resistance.

A high-quality multimeter costs about the same as a good diesel locomotive, so it may be some time before you can invest in one. In the meantime you can make a simple voltage indicator and continuity checker as shown in fig. 5-22. If the lamp lights, voltage is present. The brightness of the lamp provides an indication of the voltage. A 16-volt lamp begins to glow faintly at about 3 volts.

The continuity checker is used like an ohmmeter. If you suspect an open circuit between two points, disconnect the power to the circuit, connect one lead of the continuity checker to one end of the circuit, and connect the other lead to the other end. If the lamp lights, the circuit is complete.

James G. La Vake photo

Fig. 6-1. For more than a century steam was king on U. S. railroads. Here a 2-8-2 takes on a load of coal at New Lisbon, Wis.

Locomotives – power for your railroad

Locomotives are the most interesting equipment on a model railroad. The planning, benchwork, trackwork, and wiring all seem worthwhile when you place your favorite locomotive on the track, ease open the throttle, and watch it move over your railroad.

N scale locomotives are little gems — 1:160 reproductions of those huge behemoths which move goods and people over the vast network of track in North America. A good selection of N scale steam and diesel locomotives is available, and the selection continues to improve yearly.

To enable newcomers to N scale railroading to choose locomotives that are in agreement with the time period being modeled this chapter contains information about prototype locomotives. Facts about many popular locomotives are given in the table on pages 34-35.

The history of the U. S. railroad industry and its motive power is fascinating. Railroading is a large, complex industry that has changed tremendously over its 140-year history. Much can be learned about railroad history from books. Knowledge of modern-day railroading can also be gained through

observation. As you become involved in this hobby, you will be surprised at the amount of railroad activity that you previously overlooked.

Many types of motive power have been tried. Three major types have proved successful: the steam locomotive, the electric locomotive, and the diesel-electric locomotive.

Prototype steam locomotives

The first 100 years of railroading in this country were dominated by the steam locomotive, but steam locomotive design underwent drastic changes

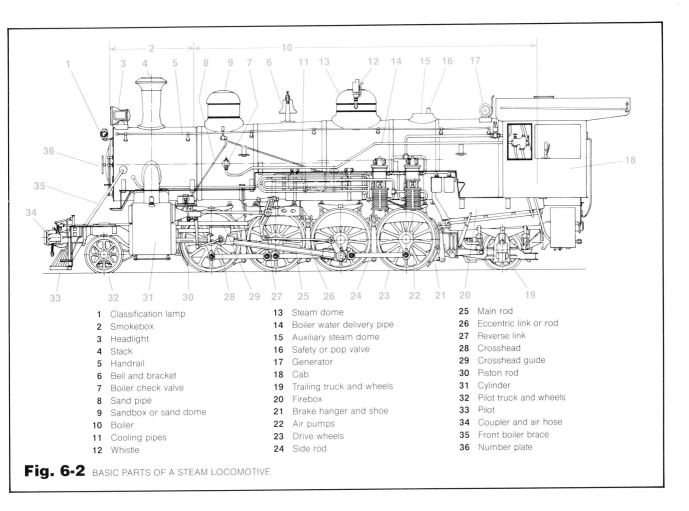

1	Classification lamp	13	Steam dome	25	Main rod
2	Smokebox	14	Boiler water delivery pipe	26	Eccentric link or rod
3	Headlight	15	Auxiliary steam dome	27	Reverse link
4	Stack	16	Safety or pop valve	28	Crosshead
5	Handrail	17	Generator	29	Crosshead guide
6	Bell and bracket	18	Cab	30	Piston rod
7	Boiler check valve	19	Trailing truck and wheels	31	Cylinder
8	Sand pipe	20	Firebox	32	Pilot truck and wheels
9	Sandbox or sand dome	21	Brake hanger and shoe	33	Pilot
10	Boiler	22	Air pumps	34	Coupler and air hose
11	Cooling pipes	23	Drive wheels	35	Front boiler brace
12	Whistle	24	Side rod	36	Number plate

Fig. 6-2 BASIC PARTS OF A STEAM LOCOMOTIVE

in those 100 years. *The Best Friend of Charleston* built in 1830 looked nothing like a Berkshire-type locomotive of 1925.

Many of the components of a steam locomotive were externally mounted and therefore important to modelers. If you can identify at least the major features of steam locomotives, you will fully appreciate the detail on your N scale models.

The external parts of a typical steam locomotive are identified in fig. 6-2. Even if you memorize all these terms, you won't be an expert on steam locomotives. The steam locomotive was a complex machine with infinite variations including a half-dozen types of valve gears, each with assorted types of mountings, and several kinds of air pumps with variations in mountings and piping arrangements. Also several different types of feedwater-heater systems existed. The arrangement of piping, and the placement and shape of so-called standard fittings, such as pilots, bells, headlights, sandboxes and steam domes, and leading and trailing trucks, were in reality not standard. Building a steam locomotive, especially an early one, was more a craft than a science. The exacting standards and mass production techniques common today were unknown to the early builders of steam locomotives.

To identify a steam locomotive, four specifications are needed: the wheel arrangement, the name of the railroad, the railroad's classification of the locomotive, and the locomotive's number.

In North America the Whyte system is used to specify wheel arrangement. The Whyte system gives the number of pilot wheels, the number of drive wheels, and then the number of trailing wheels. Written out, these numbers are separated with hyphens. For example, the locomotive shown in fig. 6-2 is a 2-8-2. Common wheel arrangements are also named; the 2-8-2 is called a Mikado. A beginner should learn some of these names so he won't be left out of the conversation when fellow model railroaders start bandying these terms about!

Each railroad's steam locomotives had distinctive characteristics. A 4-6-2 belonging to the Pennsylvania, for example, looked quite different from one owned by the Union Pacific. Additionally, each railroad had its own system of classifying its locomotives. For the most part, locomotives of the same wheel arrangement were in the same class, and usually a letter, sometimes in conjunction with a number, designated locomotive class. For example, New York Central classified some of its 4-6-4s (a Hudson-type locomotive) as J-3a's.

The locomotive's number completes the description.

Steam-servicing facilities

Prototype — Steam locomotives required complex fueling and servicing facilities. Railroad division points, usually spaced about 100 miles apart, contained facilities for fueling, washing, and repairing locomotives. By the end of the steam era, steam-locomotive design had evolved to the point where locomotives could run 1000 miles or more without major servicing. In earlier days, however, the typical run was from division point to division point and return. When a train reached a division point, the locomotive was replaced with a freshly serviced locomotive to pull the train to the next division point. At least one stop for water, and sometimes more, would have to be made between division points.

An engine usually followed a set routine when it arrived at a division point. Typically, the engine crew turned the locomotive over to a roundhouse hostler who took it down to the engine facilities. There the tender was filled with water and coal (or oil if the locomotive was an oil burner). Next, the locomotive was moved a short distance to the sand spout and sand was deposited into the large sandboxes on the top of the boiler. (These resembled domes, but sandbox is the more proper name.) Next, ashes were dumped at a pit and the running gear was washed while the

COMMON TYPES OF STEAM AND DIESEL LOCOMOTIVES

4-4-0 — American
Introduced 1840   Service: Passenger and freight
The 4-4-0 served American railroads for more than a century. It is a must on any old-time layout.

4-6-0 — Ten-Wheeler
Introduced 1847   Service: Passenger and freight
The 4-6-0 was a general-purpose engine much like the American. The last Ten-Wheelers were built in the 1920's.

2-6-0 — Mogul
Introduced 1863   Service: Freight
The Mogul primarily was a freight locomotive, although it did see some use on medium-speed passenger trains. The last Moguls were built around 1910.

4-6-2 — Pacific
Introduced 1902   Service: Passenger
The Pacific primarily was used for passenger service, but some roads also used them on freight trains. They were built until the mid 1930's and lasted until the diesels came.

0-4-0
Introduced 1830   Service: Switching
The first locomotives, such as the DeWitt Clinton, were 0-4-0's. Operation at any speed over 20 mph, though, required leading trucks to guide the locomotive into curves, and the 0-4-0 was limited to switching duties.

0-6-0
Introduced 1890   Service: Switching
The six-wheel switcher was the most common type of yard engine and appeared on the roster of nearly every railroad.

0-8-0
Introduced 1900   Service: Switching
The eight-wheel switcher was used for switching jobs too heavy for the 0-6-0. The last 0-8-0's were built in 1951.

4-8-4 — Northern
Introduced 1927   Service: Passenger and freight
The Northerns were dual-service engines, intended for fast heavy passenger and freight trains.

2-8-0 — Consolidation
Introduced 1866   Service: Freight
The Consolidation was the most popular steam locomotive design. It came in sizes ranging from the tiny "lawnmowers" used by short lines up to the massive 2-8-0's of the anthracite carriers.

2-8-2 — Mikado
Introduced 1903   Service: Freight
The 2-8-2 was the standard freight locomotive for many years. More than 10,000 were built between 1903 and 1930. Many Mikados remained in service until the end of the steam era.

4-8-2 — Mountain
Introduced 1911   Service: Passenger and freight
Designed for passenger service in mountainous territory, the 4-8-2 also pulled freight trains on many roads.

2-8-4 — Berkshire
Introduced 1925   Service: Freight
The Berkshire was the first locomotive with a practical four-wheel trailing truck, which permitted a much larger firebox that could produce more steam for hauling heavy loads at high speeds.

4-6-4 — Hudson
Introduced 1927   Service: Passenger
The Hudson created the same sensation in the passenger field that the Berkshire did in freight, hauling much heavier loads than the 4-6-2's it replaced.

4-6-6-4 — Challenger
Introduced 1936   Service: Freight
The first heavy articulated locomotive in the U. S. was an 0-6-6-0 designed for pusher service. Articulateds soon acquired leading and trailing trucks and more drivers, but for 30 years they were basically ponderous, slow-speed machines. Both the Challenger and the Big Boy (4-8-8-4) were fast engines, capable of 60 mph, and turned the articulated into a fast freight engine.

4-4-2 — Atlantic
Introduced 1896   Service: Passenger
The 4-4-2 was one of the first locomotives to use a trailing truck, which permitted a larger firebox. The last Atlantics built (1935-1937) were the streamlined ones that pulled the Milwaukee Road's Hiawatha.

EMD SW1 and NW2
Introduced 1939   Service: Switching
These were the first Electro-Motive switchers to use the 567 engine. Earlier and later EMD switchers look alike and have horsepower ratings from 600 to 1500.

EMD FTA and FTB
Introduced 1939   Service: Freight
The first FT, a four-unit 5400-h.p. model, toured the country for 11 months demonstrating that the diesel could perform as a freight locomotive. The first production models entered service in 1941.

Alco S1 and S2
Introduced 1940   Service: Switching
The 660-h.p. S1 and the 1000-h.p. S2 were built until 1950, when they were superseded by the S3 and S4, which had the same horsepower ratings.

Alco RS1
Introduced 1940
Service: Switching, light freight and light passenger
The RS1 resembled an S2 (above) on a longer underframe, with road trucks and an optional steam generator in the short hood for heating passenger cars.

EMD E7A and E7B
Introduced 1945   Service: Passenger
The 2000-h.p. E7, EMD's first postwar passenger diesel, deserves the credit for replacing steam on most of the nation's passenger trains. The E series dates from 1937; seven variations were produced before World War II and three after. The E7 was the most popular of the Es.

EMD F3A and F3B
Introduced 1945   Service: Freight
Although primarily a freight locomotive, some F3s (and F7s and F9s) were equipped with steam generators and used for passenger service. The F series, successor to the prewar FTs, included the F2s (1350 h.p.), the F3s and F7s (1500 h.p.), and the F9s (1750 h.p.).

Alco PA1 and PB1
Introduced 1946   Service: Passenger
These handsome, long-nosed 2000-h.p. and 2250-h.p. units are known as PA's (whether PA1, PA2, PA3, PB1, etc.). Passenger A units outnumbered B units because a two-unit set was too long for most turntables and the railroads therefore preferred double-ended sets.

EMD FP7
Introduced 1949   Service: Passenger
The FP7 was a lengthened version of the F7, with extra room for water tanks for the steam generator. The unit was marketed as a heavy-duty passenger locomotive.

EMD GP7
Introduced 1949
Service: Freight, passenger, and switching
The GP series (for General Purpose) of diesels ushered in a new look in diesel locomotives. They were designed to be functional rather than handsome. Geeps have grown steadily over the years; the GP40, introduced in 1965, produces 3000 h.p., twice the horsepower of the GP7.

EMD SD7
Introduced 1952
Service: Freight, passenger, and switching
The SD's (for Special Duty) are longer than their GP counterparts and ride on six-wheel, three-motor trucks. They generally were intended for lower speeds and heavier trains than the Geeps.

General Electric U25B
Introduced 1959   Service: Freight
General Electric's U series, nicknamed "U-Boats," are a functional design like EMD's Geeps and SD's. Models with a B suffix have four-wheel trucks, and models with a C suffix have six-wheel trucks.

EMD SD40-2
Introduced 1972   Service: Freight
The 3000-h.p., six axle SD40-2 units were the most popular six motor diesels of the 1970s and 80s. As with earlier EMD models, GP models have four-wheel trucks; SD models have six-wheel trucks.

General Electric Dash 8 40B
Introduced 1987   Service: Freight
The microcomputer controlled Dash 8 40B is a 4000-h.p., four-axle work horse with a utilitarian body. Like GE's U25B, the B suffix indicates four-wheel trucks and a C suffix indicates six-wheel trucks.

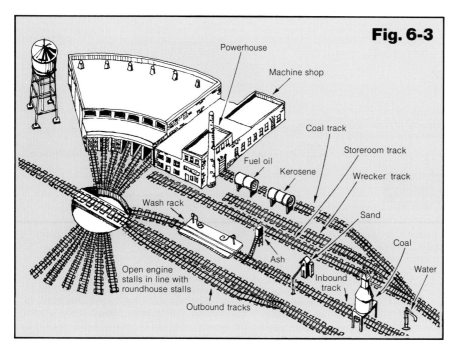

Fig. 6-3

Powerhouse

Machine shop

Coal track

Storeroom track

Fuel oil

Kerosene

Wrecker track

Wash rack

Sand

Coal

Ash

Open engine stalls in line with roundhouse stalls

Inbound track

Water

Outbound tracks

Don Hough.

Fig. 6-4. D. Simpson's layout includes a scratchbuilt turntable and roundhouse.

engine stood over a drainage grid. During or after this sequence, the engine was inspected to see if repairs were necessary. If so, the locomotive was moved into a stall in the roundhouse. If not, it was turned on the turntable, lubricated, and moved to the "ready track." The fire was banked to provide just enough steam in the boiler to maintain the locomotive in a ready state; or, if the locomotive was not going to be needed for several days, it was stored on a dead-engine track and the fire was allowed to go out.

Figure 6-3 shows a typical medium-size service facility.

N scale — All the structures necessary to model a steam-locomotive servicing facility in N scale are available in ready-built or kit form. See fig. 6-4. A service facility adds both scenic and operating interest to a model railroad, although such a facility may occupy a large area even in N scale. However, like other features on your layout, a model servicing facility can be simplified and compressed to fit in a small space and yet retain the flavor of the prototype.

Prototype diesel locomotives

The application of the internal combustion engine to railroading culminated in the development of the diesel-

electric locomotive. A diesel engine drives an electric generator whose output powers truck-mounted electric motors. The diesel locomotive entered the U. S. railroad scene in 1924; however, it did not supplant the steam locomotive until after World War Two. Our nation's railroads made the transition from steam to diesel between 1947 and 1957, although some steam locomotives continued in branchline service into the 1960s.

Diesels — being a product of our modern, standardized, mass-production-oriented technology — are easier to describe than steam locomotives. Most of the mechanical parts of a diesel are concealed under the body shell. The external parts of a typical diesel are identified in fig. 6-5. Standard models are offered by diesel manufacturers. In most cases you can completely identify a particular diesel locomotive by speci-

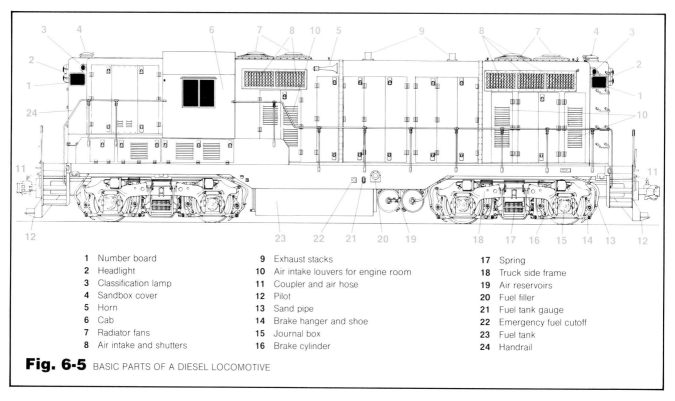

1 Number board	**9** Exhaust stacks	**17** Spring
2 Headlight	**10** Air intake louvers for engine room	**18** Truck side frame
3 Classification lamp	**11** Coupler and air hose	**19** Air reservoirs
4 Sandbox cover	**12** Pilot	**20** Fuel filler
5 Horn	**13** Sand pipe	**21** Fuel tank gauge
6 Cab	**14** Brake hanger and shoe	**22** Emergency fuel cutoff
7 Radiator fans	**15** Journal box	**23** Fuel tank
8 Air intake and shutters	**16** Brake cylinder	**24** Handrail

Fig. 6-5 BASIC PARTS OF A DIESEL LOCOMOTIVE

fying the railroad name, the manufacturer's model number, and the locomotive number.

Diesel-servicing facilities

Prototype — The change from steam to diesel power occurred primarily because the diesel required less servicing and maintenance. Modern diesels are capable of operating long distances between fuelings and even longer distances before they need major maintenance.

During the transition period from steam to diesel, diesels were refueled and serviced at steam servicing facilities. The only additions necessary were a fuel supply, fuel hoses, and a water hose. Inspection pits, wash racks, sanding towers, and even roundhouses were used in common with steam. Later, separate (though usually adjacent) facilities were built.

The essential steps in diesel servicing are inspection, refueling, and washing. The order in which these steps are performed may vary from one service facility to another, but here is a typical sequence:

The locomotive arrives at the wash area, where its trucks are cleaned. See fig. 6-7. Fueling is next. In a large complex such as this, the sand, water, and fuel devices are spaced to match the various receptacles on the diesel units. While locomotives are fueled, traction motors and running gear are inspected.

The locomotive may now be washed completely, either by hand or by a mechanical washer with rotary brushes. If repairs or other maintenance is required, the unit moves into the shops; otherwise it moves to the ready track to await its next assignment.

Many diesel lash-ups have cabs at both ends, so the units can operate in either direction and will not have to be turned at the end of a run. If it is necessary to turn a single unit, a turntable or turning track (a loop or a wye) may be used.

N scale — All the components necessary to build an N scale model of a modern diesel-servicing facility are available. See fig. 6-8. A diesel-servicing facility requires much less space on a layout than steam facilities.

N scale locomotives

Whether you prefer steam power, diesel power, or both, you will find a wide selection of N scale locomotives to choose from. Most N scale locomotives are of the ready-to-run variety and feature finely detailed plastic bodies. A sampling of the different models available at your hobby shop is shown in fig. 6-9.

Before purchasing a new locomotive to add to your motive power roster, review these five considerations:

● *Is it an appealing model?* Every item on the model need not be exactly

MODEL RAILROADER: Jim Hediger.

Fig. 6-6. Union Pacific has diesel fuel, sand, and water facilities beside its mainline tracks at La Grande, Ore., to service locomotives on through trains.

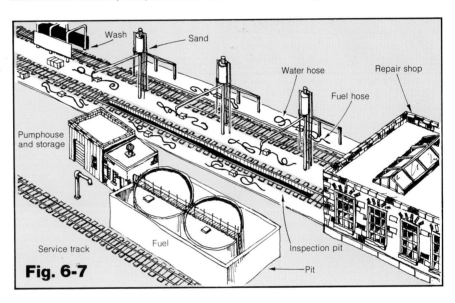

Fig. 6-7

Wash Sand Water hose Repair shop Fuel hose Pumphouse and storage Service track Fuel Inspection pit Pit

MODEL RAILROADER: A. L. Schmidt.

Fig. 6-8. Model of a small diesel service facility includes sand tower and oil tank.

scale size but the model should capture the flavor of the prototype. The overall effect is important.

● *Does it fit your layout concept?* We discussed this in Chapter 2. The locomotive should correspond to the historical setting of your layout. The information on pages 34-35 will help you

decide whether a particular model is right for your layout.

● *Will it run on your layout?* Long-wheelbase equipment will not operate properly on sharp curves. Find the minimum radius the locomotive can negotiate.

● *Is it offered in your road name?*

Models can be repainted and relettered for any road, prototype or fictitious. N scale decals and dry transfers are offered by several companies. Because locomotive models are expensive, approach major alterations with caution if you are a beginner. Learn the basics of painting plastics, first on structures, then on cars, and finally on locomotives.

• *Does it perform well?* Performance is impossible to determine by looking at the model in its case. The major model railroad magazines publish reviews of new products in every issue. Try to locate a review for the locomotive you are considering in a back issue of your magazines. Also, request a demonstration run of the model before you buy it. In general, locomotives which run well initially continue to run well. Most hobby shops that are well-stocked with model-railroad equipment will have at least a short N scale test track.

Maintenance

N scale locomotives shouldn't require much maintenance. The biggest maintenance problem I have encountered is one common to all modeling scales — dirt. Regular cleaning of the track and locomotive wheels solves most of the problem. Several brands of track-cleaning solutions are on the market. In addition to track and wheel cleaning, complete cleaning of locomotive drive mechanisms should be performed now and then.

I do not want to imply that locomotives will be maintenance free. Periodic lubrication is required and parts do deteriorate. Common items requiring occasional replacement are traction tires, motor brushes, and headlight bulbs.

Most manufacturers include at least rudimentary maintenance instructions with their locomotives. Ask your hobby shop manager if maintenance literature is available for your locomotive. If you are able to obtain a manufacturer's maintenance manual, follow its procedures and recommendations. If you'd rather not do the maintenance work yourself, take it to your hobby shop's service department. Many hobby shops do this type of work and the charges are reasonable.

Eventually, just about every model locomotive gets taken apart. There are several reasons for doing so:

• To properly lubricate the model.
• To replace an internal part that has worn out.
• To thoroughly clean the mechanism.
• To satisfy your curiosity as to how this mechanical marvel is assembled.

Before disassembly, carefully examine the model and note the relationship of the parts. As you disassemble the model, mentally note what goes where. Avoid disassembling the model any further than absolutely necessary to perform the required maintenance.

Most steam-locomotive superstructures are fastened to the chassis by a screw hidden in the sand dome or smokestack. In addition, there may be some tab-and-slot fasteners at the rear of the shell. Remove the screw and begin to gently separate the shell from the chassis. By noting the points of resistance, you can determine where other fasteners are located. Once you have the shell removed, the rest of the disassembly sequence can be determined by inspection. An exploded view of a typical N scale steam locomotive is shown in fig. 6-10. Disassemble the geared driver sets only if absolutely necessary. Correctly realigning three or four gears in reassembly is tedious and frustrating work.

The plastic shells of diesel locomotives are held to the chassis by tab-and-slot joints along the bottom edges. First remove the body from the chassis by spreading the bottom of the plastic body shell slightly (so the slots clear the tabs) and lifting the shell off the chassis as shown in fig. 6-11. The remaining disassembly sequence can be determined by inspection. An exploded view of a typical N scale diesel is shown in fig. 6-12.

It is important to lubricate your models every so often. If lubrication instructions are supplied with your model, follow them and use the recommended lubricants to comply with the conditions of the model's warranty.

If the manufacturer does not recommend any particular lubricants, select types that are compatible with plastics. Some synthetic lubricants will attack plastic and ruin a locomotive. I use No. 102 grease and No. 108 oil made by La Belle Industries. These are safe to use on plastic models.

Drive gears and the motor bearings need lubrication more than other parts. I use the La Belle grease for drive gears and the oil for motor bearings and other lubrication points. A thorough lubrication requires disassembling the locomotive far enough to expose the gearbox and the motor bearings.

On many locomotives drive gears can be adequately lubricated without disassembly. Most N scale locomotives, both steam and diesel, have gears on the center of the truck axles which mesh with a worm gear on the motor shaft. The axle gears usually are accessible from the bottom of the model. To lubricate, place the model upside down in a cushioned cradle, fig. 6-13, and apply grease sparingly to exposed gears. During operation this grease will be distributed to all mating gears. This lubrication method will not work on lo-

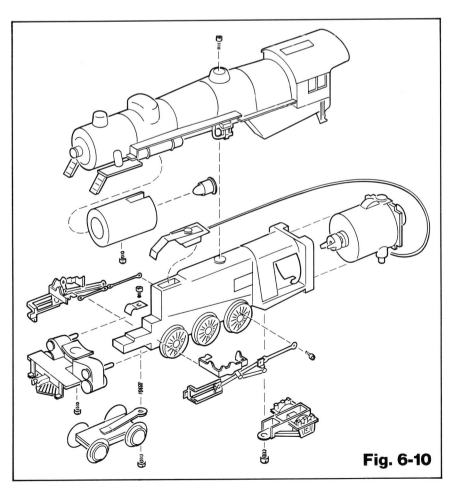

Fig. 6-9. A roundhouse/turntable scene by Dave Hannah. George Hall photo.

Fig. 6-10

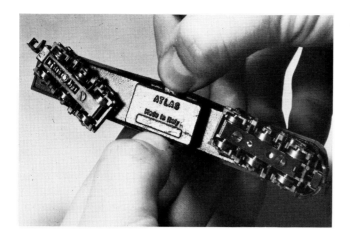

Fig. 6-11. Disassembly of N scale diesels starts by removing the body from the frame. Note the tabs on the side of the frame.

comotives whose wheels are driven from the side of the axle rather than the center. The worm gear does not directly mate with the drive gears and therefore will not receive any lubrication (some small steam switching-type locomotives have this gear arrangement).

N scale steam locomotives have other moving parts such as main rods, side rods, and valve gear. The main rods and side rods on models do not actually drive the wheels, so they are not working under any load. A little light oil applied to these points after each cleaning should be all the lubrication that will be necessary.

Apply both oil and grease sparingly. Parts that are excessively lubricated will collect dirt and cause electrical pickup problems.

Try to establish a regular lubrication schedule tailored to your type of operation. I would suggest lubricating locomotives after every 100 hours of operation or every 6 months, whichever comes first.

Some N scale locomotives, steam and diesel, are equipped with rubber traction treads on one or two sets of driving wheels. These resemble tiny rubber bands, fig. 6-14, which slip into a slot in the wheel. They give the locomotive more pulling power. Traction tires usually are found on lightweight models.

The traction tires should be replaced before they wear out completely, or operation will be affected. This is an easy procedure. Place the locomotive upside down in a cushioned cradle and pry off the tire with a small screwdriver, or cut it off with an X-acto knife. On steam locomotives the driver rod must be removed. Use a small tweezer to slip the new tire in place. Usually, disassembly is not required with diesel models. The new tire can be squeezed between the wheel and the side frame and slipped onto the wheel. See fig. 6-14.

Eventually, motor brushes also may need replacement. Motor brushes are carbon slugs that provide a sliding electrical connection between the motor terminals and the motor communicator. See fig. 6-15. The brushes are held against the commutator by a small spring. As the brush wears, the spring keeps the brush in contact with the commutator. When the brushes wear down so that they no longer are in continuous contact with the commutator, motor running becomes jerky or ceases entirely. Replace motor brushes when they wear down to about one-third their original length. Inspect the motor brushes during chassis cleaning.

Headlight lamps are easy to replace. There are numerous types of bulb installations found on models. On most,

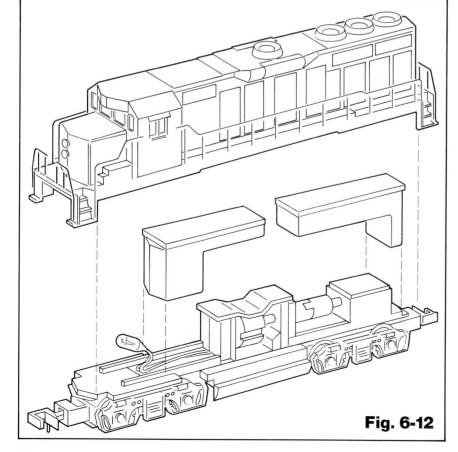

Fig. 6-12

Fig. 6-13. Apply the lubricant sparingly. In most cases applying it to one or two gears is sufficient for entire drive unit.

 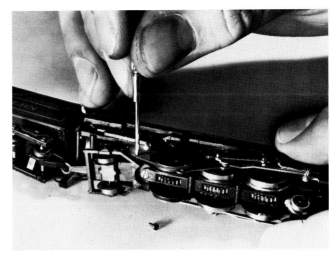

Fig. 6-14. Worn traction tires are not difficult to replace. A small pointed tool, such as a screwdriver, is usually all you need.

Fig. 6-15. Replacing worn motor brushes is a simple task which may require removing the motor from the frame.

Fig. 6-16. (Above top) Once most major cities had electrically operated streetcars. The popular PCC car was introduced in the mid-1930s in an effort to counter competition from buses. This model PCC car is by Bachmann. Fig. 6-17. (Above bottom) Electric locomotives like the model E60PH by General Electric pull Amtrak's high-speed passenger trains today in the Northeast Corridor. This model is by Bachmann.

the bulb (or bulbs) fits into some type of socket. Replacement is simply a matter of removing the locomotive body shell and snapping in a new bulb. Some models use bulbs with wire leads, and soldering is required to replace this type. Use a small soldering iron (30-40 watt) and resin-core solder.

Establish a regular cleaning schedule for locomotives just as you would for lubrication. The cleaning schedule will depend on frequency of operation, how clean the layout and layout room are kept, and whether the models are covered when not in use. An annual cleaning is sufficient for most operating conditions.

A thorough lubrication after cleaning is mandatory because cleaning fluid removes all traces of lubricants.

How about electric locomotives?

I haven't forgotten electric locomotives. This fascinating aspect of the hobby is popular in the larger modeling scales. Check with your local hobby shop to see what is available. You may want to erect overhead or install outside third rail on a portion of your layout and operate electric-locomotive-powered trains such as those found on electric railroads in the eastern U. S. In addition you might explore the field of interurbans and trolleys.

41

Fig. 7-1. Hubbard Yard handles traffic moving across the SW&P. Here, a westbound unit sulphur train of shorty tank cars is just beginning to roll. Photo by Bruce Nall.

D. McClary

Fig. 7-2. A long freight train stops to do some switching at one of the industries on Dick Taylor's Hempstead & Maryville.

Cars for freight and passengers

The railroad industry has developed an impressive array of conveyances for people, animals, goods, and raw materials. The history of the development of railroad cars is fascinating in itself. It has special significance for model railroaders who want to build and operate a realistic railroad in miniature.

Rolling stock is especially important to N scale model railroaders because we can operate so much of it. N scale is *the* operator's scale. Some N scale clubs have operated 150-car freight trains, equal in length to freights operated by modern-day railroads. In the space of the average basement, an N scale layout large enough to operate 40- to 60-car trains can be built. Even apartment dwellers and others with only limited space can build an N scale model railroad large enough to operate 15- to 25-car trains.

In Chapter 6 I pointed out the tremendous changes locomotive design has undergone in the 140 years of railroad history in this country. Likewise,

the rolling stock has changed dramatically. New types of cars are continually being developed so that railroads can better serve their customers and attract new business. In addition, many changes have been made to existing cars in the interest of comfort and safety. In order to select cars that fit the concept of your layout, you must know a little about the development of railroad rolling stock. I hope that the information presented in this chapter will inspire you to pursue the subject in more depth on your own.

Freight cars

When you stop your car at a grade crossing to wait for a freight train to pass, you probably notice the variety of cars operated by today's railroads. N scale models of some common freight cars are shown in fig. 7-3. Many other cars also are offered in N scale. Check at your local hobby shop.

Freight car markings — You can tell a lot about a freight car from its mark-

ings. Here are explanations of the standard abbreviations. CAPY — capacity, in pounds; LD LMT — load limit, in pounds; EXW — extreme width; EW — eaves width; IL — inside length; IW — inside width; IH — inside height; CU FT — cubic-foot capacity; BLT — date built.

A typical freight train — It is difficult to describe a typical freight train. A freight train's size and makeup depend on the type of service it provides and the historical and geographical setting it operates in. However, we can describe some elements of the train.

Freight cars are owned by the railroads, by shippers, and by private companies, such as REA Express, Trailer Train, and Fruit Growers Express. To make transcontinental shipments faster and less expensive, railroads have interchange agreements which enable shipments to be made anywhere in the country in the same cars. Because of this interchange of cars, a typical freight includes cars of various railroads and private owners.

Bringing up the rear of almost every freight train is a caboose. This car is a traveling office for the conductor and the crew. From the vantage point of a cupola or a bay window the crew keeps close watch on the cars during the trip. The freight train's caboose nearly always belongs to the railroad operating the train. Therefore, the locomotive and caboose on your N scale freight trains must be painted and lettered for the same railroad, unless your railroad "pools" motive power and cabooses with its connections. The cars between the locomotive and caboose may be of almost any type and lettered for almost any railroad as long as they are historically correct for the time period you are modeling. Modern jumbo cars, for instance, don't belong behind a steam locomotive.

Selecting freight cars that belong — The selection of modern N scale freight cars enables model railroaders to duplicate almost any railroad freight operation of recent years. Modeling the old railroads, however, is hampered by a limited selection of rolling stock. If you are interested in modeling the "good old days" of railroading, check at your

Fig. 7-3. Industries at Hagerstown line both sides of the joint Pennsylvania-Norfolk & Western Shomo Yard. The Carroll Shoe Co. building is from Magnuson Models, while the Landis Tool Co. is a modified AHM kit. A. L. Schmidt photo.

local hobby shop to see what type of old-time equipment is available.

If you model the pre-1900 era of railroading, you won't need a big layout or a lot of equipment to build and operate a realistic railroad. Trains were short and slow in those days. A typical 15- to 20-car freight traveling at 20 to 25 mph with numerous stops along the way would be lucky to cover 100 miles in a day.

To operate in an authentic manner, select freight cars that fit the time setting of your layout. Freight cars have changed substantially over the last 100 years. Some of the major changes are noted in fig. 7-4. Here are some other changes to consider when selecting freight cars for your layout:

Trucks are the frames and pairs of wheels which support each end of the car. The components of a freight truck are identified in fig. 7-5. Many different types of trucks have been used under freight cars over the years. The four most common types are woodbeam, archbar, Andrews, and Bettendorf or AAR standard.

Wood-beam truck: This early design's name was derived from the fact that the principal components of the truck were hardwood beams. Woodbeam trucks such as the one shown in fig. 7-6 were standard until about 1860.

Archbar truck: This early all-metal truck was much stronger than the wood-beam. The side frames were made of individual metal straps held together with long bolts. The journal boxes were separate parts. The design was subject to metal fatigue and subsequent failure of the truck. With the development of heavy-duty cast-side frame trucks in 1903, the days of the archbar truck were numbered. In 1938 the Interstate Commerce Commission banned the use of archbar trucks on cars that were operated in interchange service.

Andrews truck: This heavy-duty truck with cast side frames was used during the changeover period from archbar to Bettendorf trucks. An important feature of the Andrews truck was that journal boxes from discarded archbar trucks could be used in the Andrews frame.

Bettendorf truck: The Bettendorf Company made this one-piece cast-side frame truck with integral journal boxes in 1903. From this development evolved a new family of stronger, better-riding trucks. Although a number of competitive designs similar in principle to the Betten-

dorf were used, the Bettendorf design was made standard by the Association of American Railroads and is the principal type in use today. Newer trucks usually have roller bearings instead of friction bearings. Friction bearing trucks contain the traditional journal box lid. Roller bearing trucks contain a sealed journal box.

Brakes — Early freight cars contained hand brakes, which were applied by turning a brake wheel that extended above the roof at the end of each car. To stop a train, the engineer gave a whistle signal to the brakemen, who climbed to the top of the cars and ran along the roofwalk setting the brakes. See fig. 7-7. The engineer also applied steam-operated locomotive brakes, and for emergency stops he put the locomotive in reverse. Needless to say, stopping a train in those days was a lengthy process, planned well in advance if possible.

A typical hand-brake system, called the Elder brake, is shown in fig. 7-8.

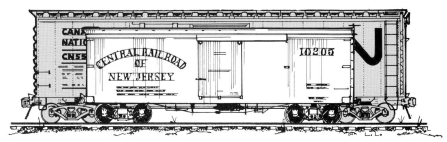

Fig. 7-4. Compare the 36-foot wood box car of 1900 with today's 50-foot steel box car.

This type was in common use around 1880.

George Westinghouse obtained a patent for his air-brake system, called the straight air brake, in 1869. Compressed air traveled from a reservoir on the locomotive to brake cylinders on each car. This worked well on short trains, but on long trains the time lag was too great. Also, if there was a leak anywhere in the system the brakes would not operate.

Later Westinghouse developed the automatic air-brake system. With this system each car is equipped with an air reservoir which must be pumped up to a certain pressure before the brakes can be released. A valve, called the triple valve, on each car controls the brake application in accordance with the train-line pressure, which is controlled by the engineer. By having a supply of air on each car, the response to an application of the brakes is quickened. The brakes of the automatic air-brake system are set by lowering the air pressure rather than by raising it. Therefore, if a leak should occur in the system, the car brakes will be set automatically.

The general arrangement of the Westinghouse brake system with a type-K valve is shown in fig. 7-9. This brake system was used from just before 1920 until the early 1930s.

The AB system was adopted as standard by the AAR in 1933. This system has a different control valve, type AB, and a larger air reservoir. The three main components — air reservoir, brake cylinder, and control valve are arranged as shown in fig. 7-10.

When reliable automatic train brakes of the K and AB types were developed, the importance of the hand brake diminished. The brake wheel was mounted on a short horizontal shaft on the end of the car on cars built after 1920. If you model the post-1920 era, your cars should have modern end-mounted brake wheels. On the newest cars, the brake wheel is mounted low on the end of the car, eliminating the need for the trainman to climb a ladder.

Couplers — Two types of couplers, link-and-pin and knuckle, have been used on U. S. railroads. The link-and-pin was used during the first 60 years of railroading and variations of the knuckle have been used since then. Couplers are discussed in Chapter 8.

Passenger cars

Many model railroaders do not include passenger operations in their layouts. This is unfortunate because passenger trains can be as much fun to operate as freight trains, and until recently they were an important part of the railroad scene. Before the advent of the superhighway and the jetliner, passenger trains were *the* way to travel. Now, with the help of Amtrak, travelers are once again discovering the passenger train.

On May 1, 1971, 20 U. S. railroads turned their intercity passenger business over to the National Railroad Passenger Corp., better known as Amtrak. Amtrak was established by an Act of Congress to save the intercity passenger service which the railroads, because of heavy operating losses, could

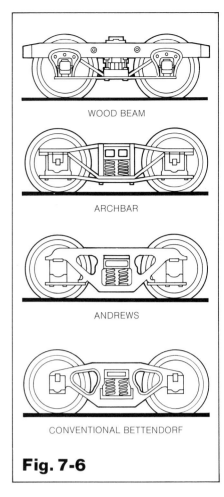

WOOD BEAM

ARCHBAR

ANDREWS

CONVENTIONAL BETTENDORF

Fig. 7-6

no longer afford to operate. Amtrak bought passenger equipment from the railroads, eliminated duplication of services, and advertised train travel with its slogan "We're making the trains worth traveling again." Amtrak became important to modelers because the appearance of passenger trains was affected.

Before Amtrak, the passenger trains of each railroad wore a uniform paint scheme and the cars were designed to be operated as a uniform-looking train.

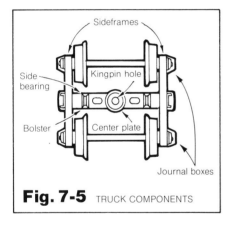

Fig. 7-5 TRUCK COMPONENTS

Sideframes

Side bearing

Kingpin hole

Bolster

Center plate

Journal boxes

Fig. 7-12. The makeup of a passenger train is determined by the distance to be traveled and the type of service offered. Here are consists for three common types of passenger trains.

COMMUTER TRAIN

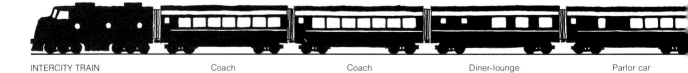

INTERCITY TRAIN   Coach   Coach   Diner-lounge   Parlor car

LONG-HAUL LUXURY TRAIN   Baggage-mail   Baggage-dormitory

Fig. 7-7. Until the advent of air brakes, muscle power was needed to stop trains.

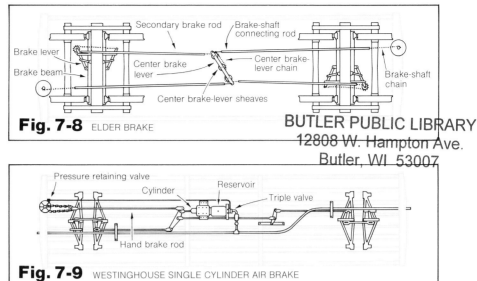

Fig. 7-8 ELDER BRAKE

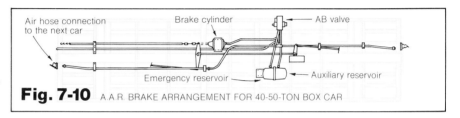

Fig. 7-9 WESTINGHOUSE SINGLE CYLINDER AIR BRAKE

Fig. 7-10 A.A.R. BRAKE ARRANGEMENT FOR 40-50-TON BOX CAR

Many trains were downright beautiful.

Today's Amtrak matched consists (the make-up of the train) stainless steel cars with their red, white, and blue striping are attractive. However, during the transition period a hodge-podge of equipment in various railroad color schemes could be seen around the country. If you decide to model this Amtrak transition period, you can operate just about any combination of passenger equipment and be in agreement with the prototype.

Before Amtrak, U. S. passenger trains were operated by the individual railroads. Let's review pre-Amtrak train service.

Passenger trains were once the pride of each railroad company. They were well maintained, assigned the best motive power, and given superiority over freights on the timetables. The best passenger trains of the railroad were named — *Super Chief, Empire Builder, Broadway Limited* — and had a character of their own. These name trains normally carried sleeping cars, dining and lounge cars, and an observation car. Some carried priority mail, and a few were so exclusive that they did not carry coaches — "First-class passengers only." Less exalted trains performed the homely tasks of carrying mail, express, and local passengers and transporting commuters to and from work. Their consists reflected their duties: The locals carried coaches, baggage cars, mail cars, and possibly express refrigerator cars for perishables; commuter trains carried high-capacity coaches; and intercity expresses carried coaches, a diner or lounge car, and perhaps a parlor car for the first-class trade. Some typical passenger train consists are shown in fig. 7-12.

Selecting passenger cars — A good selection of passenger cars is available in N scale. If you want to ensure that the equipment you select is 100 percent authentic, you will have to do a little research on the equipment operated by your favorite railroad. Most model railroad manufacturers design fairly accurate models of one railroad's distinctive passenger equipment but offer it also in paint schemes for other railroads which may never have operated anything even similar in appearance. This practice is also true of diesel locomotives and many of the steam locomotive designs which were unique to a particular railroad. Reviews of new products in the model railroad magazines often note these points.

During the past 100 years three methods of construction have been used for passenger cars. Until the turn of the century passenger cars were built of wood. Vestibules came into use in the 1880s, permitting easy passage from car to car. The first all steel passenger cars were built in the early 1900s, and heavyweight (80-90 tons) riveted steel cars were the standard for 30 years. In 1934 Union Pacific's *City of Salina* and Burlington's *Zephyr* ushered in the streamlined era. Welding replaced riveting, aluminum and stainless steel replaced steel, and the weight per car was cut to 60 tons or so.

Railroads have been reluctant to scrap cars just because they are old. Wooden passenger cars remained in service through World War Two, although mainly in branchline and suburban service. Heavyweight sleeping cars operated in the Pullman fleet until

Fig. 7-11. Like so many before it, the Amtrak passenger train's color scheme is distinctive — and attractive.

coach   Dome coach   Diner   Sleeper   Dome observation

Fig. 7-13. The Crandic's Union Station is free-lanced, but loosely based on the Denver & Rio Grande's station at Salt Lake City. The builder worked from a photo in Edwin P. Alexander's book, *Down at the Depot.* All the structures seen here were scratchbuilt from cardboard. The Santa Fe PA-1 is by Con-Cor; Pennsy E8 by Atlas. Jim Hediger photo.

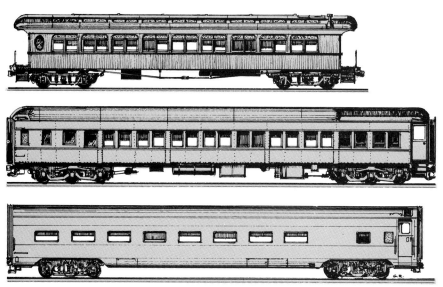

Fig. 7-14. The three types of passenger car construction are illustrated here: wood, heavyweight steel, and lightweight, streamlined steel.

the mid-1960s in the U. S., and heavyweight coaches, diners, and head-end cars ran right up to the advent of Amtrak. Your choice of cars for passenger service is a wide one, no matter which period of time you set your model in. Figure 7-14 shows some of the significant changes that have taken place as the passenger car has evolved.

Maintenance-of-way equipment

In addition to the revenue equipment operated by railroads, a variety of rolling stock is needed to maintain the right of way. This equipment includes track maintenance machines, snowplows, wreck cranes, and cars to carry supplies and house the workers.

Not much equipment of this type is offered commercially for model railroads, but the realism of every layout could benefit from the inclusion of a few pieces of this equipment. If you enjoy building your own models, consider including maintenance-of-way equipment on your layout.

Keep 'em rolling

Whether or not you select or build rolling stock that is 100 percent authentic, you will always want to keep your rolling stock in good running condition. Most ready-to-run N scale rolling stock is virtually maintenance-free. Following is a brief listing of the key elements involved in trouble-free operation, and the type of attention they may require.

Wheels — When an accumulation of crud builds up on the wheels of your rolling stock, remove it with the same cleaning solvent you use to clean your track.

Wheel bearings — A typical N scale wheel set has metal axles which terminate in needlepoint bearings. These bearings fit into side frame "journal boxes" which are made of a slippery plastic called Delrin. This combination results in a free-rolling truck. I have found that lubricating these bearings is not necessary and in fact the lubricant creates problems because it catches dust.

Wheel gauge — Wheel sets occasionally get out of gauge and cause derailments. If a particular car begins to give you trouble, check to see if the wheels are in gauge. Kadee Products makes a versatile gauge, the MT-1055, which can be used to check wheel and track gauge. Wheel sets are easy to put back in gauge. One wheel of each set is insulated by a small plastic bushing in the center of the wheel. This insulated wheel can be moved back and forth on the axle. First remove the wheel set from the truck by gently spreading the side frames. Then, using two chainnosed pliers, slowly slide the wheel on the axle until it is in gauge. Be careful not to damage the needlepoint axle bearings.

Coupling cars together

Two types of couplers, each with numerous variations, have been used by U. S. railroads — the link and pin type, shown in fig. 8-2, and the knuckle type, shown in fig. 8-3.

The link and pin coupler was used during the first 50 to 60 years of railroading in this country. It was not automatic; the coupling pin had to be dropped in place by a trainman at the moment the link was in proper position. Needless to say, this was dangerous work.

In the 1880s railroads started converting to the knuckle-type automatic coupler invented by Eli Janney. The knuckle coupler is still in use today. With it both coupling and uncoupling can be done safely. The couplers mate automatically. Uncoupling is done by moving a lever on the end of the car.

N scale couplers

Two types of N scale couplers are offered: the Rapido coupler and the Kadee coupler. See fig. 8-1. The advantages and disadvantages of each type are compared in the table, left.

Rapido couplers — All N scale equipment (except that offered by Kadee) comes equipped with Rapido-style couplers, which are simple in design and reliable in operation. The couplers have a pointed front edge and are free to pivot up and down. When two couplers meet, one coupler rides up over the other and then falls in place.

To uncouple cars, one coupler must be lifted over the other. This procedure can be done manually by lifting up one

A COMPARISON OF FEATURES OF RAPIDO AND KADEE COUPLERS		
FEATURE	RAPIDO	KADEE
Cost per car	Free, included with each piece of equipment.	$.75 minimum, more for many special installations.
Installation	Ready to run with all equipment.	Requires a moderate amount of skill in all cases, and a considerable amount for special conversions.
Coupling	Good under all conditions including curves, although cars must be banged together with considerable force at times.	Excellent under all conditions including curves down to 11″ radius. Cars couple gently with just a nudge. Reliable operation is totally dependent on precise installation.
Uncoupling	Fair under all conditions including curves. Lifting action of ramp occasionally derails cars.	Excellent on straight track, poor or impossible on curves. No physical contact is made between equipment and ramp. Reliable operation is totally dependent on precise installation.
Appearance	Very poor.	Good.
Ramp Operation	Cars can uncouple only at ramp location.	Delayed feature allows cars to be spotted anywhere beyond ramp, overcoming the problem of uncoupling on curves in most cases.
Ramp cost	About $3.00 per ramp.	About $.75 per ramp. Delay feature allows fewer ramps than with Rapido.
Reliability	Generally good.	Generally excellent provided couplers are precisely installed. Unscheduled uncoupling is a major problem with fixed ramps, but can be overcome with electromagnetic or movable ramps.
Best feature	Furnished ready to use.	Smooth, reliable operation.
Worst drawback	Appearance.	Unscheduled uncoupling.

All photos, MODEL RAILROADER: A. L. Schmidt.
Fig. 8-1. Two types of N scale couplers are offered: the Kadee Magne-Matic coupler, left, and the Rapido-style coupler, right.

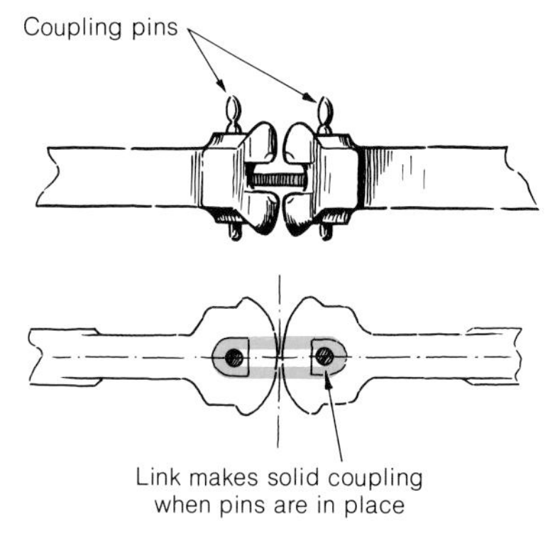

Coupling pins

Link makes solid coupling when pins are in place

Fig. 8-2 LINK AND PIN COUPLERS

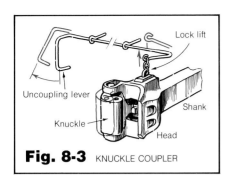

Fig. 8-3 KNUCKLE COUPLER

(Labels in figure: Lock lift, Uncoupling lever, Knuckle, Shank, Head)

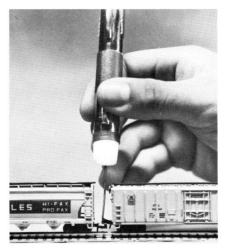

Fig. 8-4. A short length of wire taped to a penlight makes a handy uncoupling tool that helps you see what you are doing.

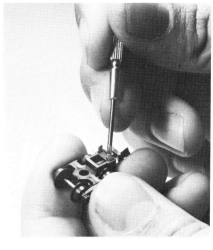

Fig. 8-5. To replace a Rapido coupler, first remove the retaining plate which is held in place by two small tabs.

end of one car. This method is unsatisfactory because of the difficulty in rerailing the car after uncoupling. A better manual method entails using a short length of wire with a small hook on one end to lift one coupler over the other without lifting the end of the car off the rails. If you tape the wire to a small penlight, you have a handy uncoupling tool that helps you see what you're doing. See fig. 8-4.

Cars equipped with Rapido couplers can also be uncoupled over an uncoupling ramp consisting of a plunger with a small shoe on top. Each coupler has a small pin extending downward and positioned slightly off-center. When the ramp, also positioned off-center between the rails, is activated, the shoe rises and contacts the pin of one coupler. Cars must be spotted exactly over the ramp to be uncoupled.

B & R Industries manufactures an electrically operated uncoupling ramp that can be used with any brand of track and installed anywhere on the layout.

Occasionally, after a derailment or — heaven forbid — a drop on the floor, a car's coupler may be broken or bent so it no longer works properly. Replacement is easy. See fig. 8-5.

Kadee couplers — Kadee Quality Products has available an automatic coupler, called the Magne-Matic, which can be fitted to any N scale car or locomotive. Both in appearance and in operation this coupler, fig. 8-1, is similar to the prototype knuckle coupler.

Because Kadee couplers look and operate like the prototype, most serious N scale modelers eventually convert all their equipment to Kadees. Kadee also manufactures N scale, which can be purchased with Magne-Matics installed.

The coupler, including the shank, is split into two horizontal layers: The knuckle is attached to the top half and the remainder of the coupler head is attached to the lower half of the shank. The couplers open and close with a scissors action. When two couplers are pushed together, the knuckles spread and engage.

Uncoupling is accomplished by stopping the cars over a special magnetic uncoupling ramp (also sold by Kadee). Each coupler has a curved metal uncoupling pin extending downward. When a

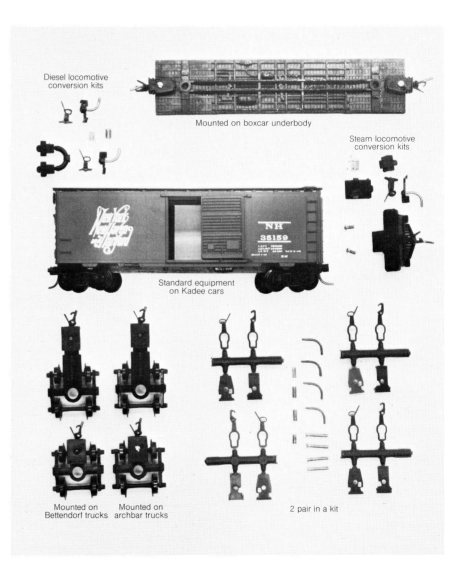

(Labels in figure: Diesel locomotive conversion kits; Mounted on boxcar underbody; Steam locomotive conversion kits; Standard equipment on Kadee cars; Mounted on Bettendorf trucks; Mounted on archbar trucks; 2 pair in a kit)

Fig. 8-6. Kadee couplers may be purchased in several different configurations.

train stops, the couplers "take slack"; on those that are over the specially polarized uncoupling ramp, the pins are moved sideways by the ramp's magnetic field. If the couplers are in tension as they pass over a ramp, the hooked shape of the knuckles prevents uncoupling.

Delayed uncoupling is another feature of the Magne-Matics. A single ramp can serve several locations.

The Kadee coupler is offered in several forms: See fig. 8-6.

Roger Baker.

Fig. 9-1. Master some basic scenery construction methods and build a fine layout like Roger Baker's Rocky Coast Line.

Scenery made simple

The appearance of a layout changes quickly and dramatically as scenery is added. No matter how sturdy the benchwork, how fine the trackwork, and how realistic the rolling stock, a layout is uninteresting without scenery.

A common misconception is that you need to have artistic ability to build great-looking scenery. Artistic talent definitely is an asset, but certainly not a requirement. Anyone can build realistic scenery using any of the common methods to form the terrain and color it.

Building terrain

A number of methods have been developed over the years to build the basic scenic form for the hills, mountains, and valleys on a layout. Older methods do not necessarily become obsolete as new techniques are developed. I'd suggest you familiarize yourself with the different methods of building the scenic form and select the one that you like best. I'll briefly describe two methods and then concentrate a little more on a third one.

Plaster over screen wire. One of the older methods of making the basic

scenic forms is the plaster over screen wire system. Screen wire is tacked or stapled to plywood formers cut to the shape of the hill or mountain you're building and then plaster is troweled onto and into the screen wire. While this method takes longer than the hard-shell method, which we'll discuss in a moment, it is a more precise way to shape the terrain and also a good method for people who are allergic to plaster and don't want to be dipping their hands in it to build hard-shell terrain.

Stacked Styrofoam. Extruded Styrofoam is used in the building trades for insulation. It comes in 4 x 8-foot sheets that are 1″ or 2″ thick and either blue or pink colors. The foam is lightweight and can be shaped easily. The pieces can be stacked up and joined with a water-soluble contact cement and then shaped with a Surfoam tool. When shaping the Styrofoam many tiny particles become airborne so it is important to wear a dust mask. Styrofoam scenic forms are ideally suited for Ntrak modules. This method is explained in Chapter 14, "Let's Build an Ntrak Module."

Hard-shell terrain. The quickest and

All photos, unless otherwise indicated, A. L. Schmidt.

Fig. 9-2. Commence your hard-shell terrain construction by mixing Hydrocal. Work in small batches, adding plaster to water.

easiest way to build good-looking scenery for a permanent home or club layout is the hard-shell method. Let's look at the steps required to build scenery using this method in more detail.

Fig. 9-3. Lay plaster-soaked paper towel strips on top of a supporting web made of masking tape and crumpled newspaper.

Fig. 9-4. Always wet hardened plaster or Hydrocal before applying a fresh coat of plaster, and before dusting on dry colors.

A rough contour for the scenery is formed by weaving a web of masking tape and crumpled newspapers. Plaster-soaked paper towels are draped over the web in a crisscross manner. The plaster sets, forming a thin but strong scenery shell.

Materials required — You will need newspapers, masking tape, thumbtacks, paper cups, paper towels, plaster, and a glass or plastic mixing bowl.

I use Scott single-fold, wet-strength paper towels, a type commonly used in public rest rooms. Such towels are not readily available in grocery stores, but you might be able to buy a case (15 packages) through a paper supply house and split it with fellow model railroaders. If you can't obtain these tough towels, try the one-ply towels sold in rolls in grocery stores.

Several types of plaster can be used. Hydrocal is a very strong plaster and I recommend using it to form the basic hard shell. Hydrocal is available through cement dealers in 100-pound bags and from some lumberyards. Certain hobby shops may sell smaller quantities of Hydrocal.

Molding plaster should be used for the final layer of hard-shell terrain after the basic Hydrocal shell has been constructed. Incidentally, if you can't locate Hydrocal, the entire job can be done with molding plaster, although a thicker application of molding plaster will be necessary for the basic shell.

Plaster of Paris works almost as well as molding plaster. Generally, it is the easiest type of plaster to find packaged in small quantities.

Preparation — Cover anything you don't want splattered by stray plaster. Use masking tape to cover all track on the layout. The control panel and the floor of the layout room should be cov-

Fig. 9-6. After the final plaster layer sets, apply layers of colored dyes to areas not to be covered by zip texturing.

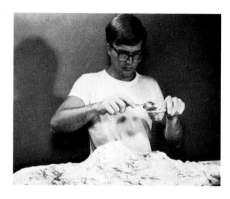

Fig. 9-7. Using a kitchen sieve sprinkle a mixture of earth-colored pigment and dry plaster over the dampened plaster.

ered with newspapers. Place an old rug at the door of the layout room to wipe plaster dust from your shoes as you leave. Plaster will be tracked all over the house if you are not careful.

The supporting shell — A flimsy web of masking tape and crumpled newspaper are all that's needed. See

Fig. 9-5. Brush molding plaster onto the Hydrocal shell. On the final layer, the brush strokes will simulate rock strata.

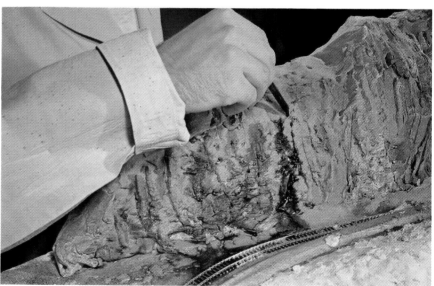

MODEL RAILROADER, Linn H. Westcott.

Fig. 9-8. Sift a grass mixture of different shades of green pigment and dry plaster over the "soil" to complete zip texturing; allow soil to show through at spots. Erosion effects can be simulated by applying dyes to grass and rocks with an eyedropper.

fig. 9-3. After the plaster hard-shell terrain becomes self-supporting, the masking tape/newspaper support may be removed.

Sometimes you may find it easier to cut cardboard profiles for terrain such as mountainous sections rather than using a tape web. Also, you may find that additional 1" x 1" scenery supports may be needed to achieve the web shape you desire. Plaster adheres very well to wood, so don't cover the ends of scenery supports with masking tape. Allow the wood posts to support the plaster directly. Hydrocal plaster sets quickly, so mix small batches. Mix 2 cups Hydrocal with 1 cup water. Pour water into the mixing bowl first and then add the plaster to the water. See fig. 9-2. A rubber spatula can be used for blending, but I prefer to use my hands. You will be covered with plaster before you're through, so don't be afraid to dig right in.

After the plaster is mixed, pull a strip of paper towel through the plaster mix, soaking both sides. Drape and overlap the towels over the newspaper and webbing. See fig. 9-3.

I recommend cleaning the mixing bowl between batches. Hardened plaster in the mixing bowl is one of the many factors that affect the setting time of plaster — it speeds up the setting process. I keep a large bowl of water on hand for cleaning the mixing bowl and rinsing my hands.

Do not be too concerned with the placement of the towel strips and its affect on the overall appearance of the terrain. The initial layer of hard-shell terrain, the Hydrocal, probably will be ragged, but the applications of molding plaster will reduce roughness.

Molding plaster can be smeared on with your hand or applied with a paintbrush or a wallpaper-paste brush. This plaster will smooth some of the undesirable bumps of the supporting shell. Also, dry colors used in zip texturing are absorbed more readily by molding plaster than by bare Hydrocal. Always wet hardened plaster before applying a fresh coat. A window-cleaner sprayer is handy for this. See fig. 9-5.

If you are not satisfied with some portion of the terrain, change it: Scenery can be raised by placing wadded newspaper on the hard shell and draping plaster-soaked towels over the newspaper. If you wish to lower scenery below the existing hard shell, get out the hammer and chisel.

Coloring methods

Many methods have also been developed to color scenery. These include using real dirt and sand, the zip texturing method, and the water-soluble method.

The water-soluble method. This method is the one most commonly used by today's model railroaders and it is fully described in Dave Frary's

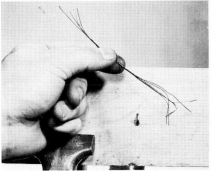
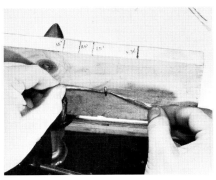
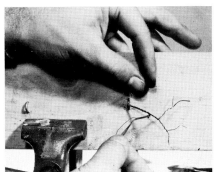
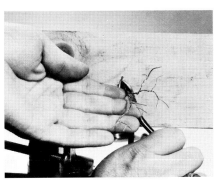

Fig. 9-9. Here is one way to mass produce trees. First, cut wires to various lengths and loosely twist together. Slip wires through a staple, fold and twist together to form tree trunk. Spread wire ends as shown to form "branches." Now snip the wire tree from the staple. Paint the trunks and limbs a blackish brown and add foliage. Foliage can be simulated with lichen or with ground foam glued to a steel wool net.

book, *How to Build Realistic Model Railroad Scenery* (Kalmbach). Basically, the method involves sprinkling various shades and grades of ground foam over wet latex paint that has been brushed over the plaster or Styrofoam scenic form. Scenic highlights and rock coloring is done using acrylic paints. This is the scenery coloring and texturing method described by Dick

Christianson in Chapter 14, "Let's Build an Ntrak Module."

I'm going to furnish an overview of an older coloring method called zip texturing that is still a good way to color a lot of terrain quickly and inexpensively. Zip texturing could be used for scenic areas in the background of a layout with a water-soluble method used for the foreground areas. Or

Fig. 9-10. Trees are easy to "plant" on your N scale layout. Simply drill a hole in the terrain and glue the tree in place.

some features of the two methods could be combined depending upon your preferences

For example, vertical rock surfaces could be stained using Rit dyes while you use the water-soluble method for other parts of the scenery. Or you could use the zip texturing process and then sprinkle on ground foam for added realism and affix it by spraying on a diluted solution of matte medium.

Let's review the steps of the zip texturing process, which is what I used for coloring the scenery on the E, Z, & Kwick layout featured in Chapter 11.

Zip texturing. Zip texturing is a process of coloring plaster scenery by dusting dry colors onto wet plaster. With this method, you can realistically simulate rock, loose soil, and grass. Dyes and dry pigment colors or temperas are all that is required.

Rit, Tintex, and similar brands of dyes work fine. Yellow, cardinal red, pagoda red, marine blue, and black are commonly used colors. Purchase them in powdered form.

The dry pigments are used to simulate earth, grass, and other scenic effects. Powdered temperas also may be employed. If your hobby shop does not stock these scenery supplies, check your local hardware store or art supply house. Six pigment colors recommended in *Scenery for Model Railroads* by Bill McClanahan are: medium yellow, raw sienna, burnt sienna, raw umber, burnt umber, and dark green.

Zip texturing involves five basic steps:
• Coat the terrain surface with a batter of molding plaster.
• Carve the molding plaster to form rock strata and other detail.
• Apply colored dyes.
• Apply a mixture of powdered pigments and dry plaster to the dampened plaster terrain.

• Squirt water onto the pigment coating to create erosion effects.

The final coat of plaster over the hard-shell terrain is necessary if you wish to carve extra detail in your landscaping. If you brush this layer on, the direction of the brush strokes can simulate stratified rock. Carve other detail into the plaster while it is setting; use an X-acto knife or other sharp tool. The dye can be sprayed, sprinkled, or poured onto the surfaces after plaster has set. See fig. 9-6. Use several applications of much diluted dye rather than one layer of strong color. Blacks, browns, and reds especially should be diluted. Rock varies in coloring, so apply more than one color over rock faces; more here, a little less there. It is not necessary to dye all surfaces, but be sure to apply dye to all *vertical* surfaces; dry powdered pigments will not cling to and conceal vertical or nearly vertical landscaping.

After the plaster has been dyed, the surface is wetted again and the dry earth sifted on. Burnt sienna and medium yellow look natural when mixed. I use the old mix-and-try method to arrive at a desirable shade of brown. This mixture should include about 25 percent molding plaster. (The molding plaster will cause the color mixture to adhere to plaster terrain surface.) Complete the dusting process in the following manner:

Wet the plaster thoroughly, using a window-cleaner sprayer containing a solution of water and a few drops of liquid detergent.

Pour some of the earth-color mixture into a medium-mesh kitchen sieve. Hold the sieve over the wet plaster and gently tap the sieve as shown in fig. 9-7.

Spray on more water until the earth mixture is moist but not wetted. Now sift some grass mixture over the "soil" (grass is made just like soil, but with an olive-green mixture of color and dry plaster).

With a small brush, touch up any small areas missed. Another method useful for touching up is directing dry color to the missed area with a small funnel. As a final step, apply dyes with an eyedropper to create special effects as shown in fig. 9-8.

Other scenic features

Structures — Structures are such an important element in layout planning and construction that I have devoted an entire chapter to the subject. Structures should be selected before scenery construction to enable you to plan for their sites before building your hard-shell terrain. Buildings should not be attached to the layout until landscaping is complete. Sometimes plaster will have to be added around building foundations to blend them into the surroundings; some color touch-up also may be necessary.

Trees — Model trees can be purchased in ready-to-plant N scale size at your hobby shop. Some N scale trees are realistic, especially the pines. Many HO scale trees are suitable for N scale. Ready-made trees can become expensive since several of them should be included on even a small layout. If you plan to use a large number of them, I would suggest building some of your own. One method of tree construction is outlined in fig. 9-9.

Trees are easy to install: Drill a hole into the hard shell where you want to "plant" a tree. A hand drill does a clean job because the plaster powder is left in a neat pile around the hole. A motor tool or electric drill is faster but scatters the plaster around, requiring a little more vacuuming. Squirt a small amount of white glue into the hole and onto the end of the tree trunk. Insert the tree in the hole. If necessary add some shims so the tree stands reasonably straight. See fig. 9-10. Let the glue dry overnight and then touch up the base of the tree.

Roads — Gravel roads can be simulated with N scale ballast. The route of the road should be fairly level. Apply the "gravel" and bond it in place using the bonded ballast method outlined in Chapter 4.

Masonite or styrene can be used for asphalt and concrete highways, streets, and sidewalks. In most cases, I use thin (about .020") styrene, because it is easy to work with and the finished road is neat and smooth. The styrene can be glued to the plaster terrain with a white glue. After the glue dries, fill in the highway shoulders with molding plaster and touch up with color. Paint the styrene a light gray to simulate concrete or dark gray to simulate asphalt.

Water — Many materials can be used to simulate water on a model railroad including: shellacked plaster, ripple glass, real water, silicone rubber, and casting resin. The two materials I have had the best results with are silicone rubber and casting resin. Silicone rubber works very well but it is expensive, so I don't recommend it for any major pours. Casting resin, a relatively inexpensive material used by craft people, works well, but it has a powerful odor and the fumes can be dangerous. Always work in a well-ventilated area and follow the manufacturer's precautions.

Other details — Scenic details distinguish an outstanding layout from a mediocre one. You can add many details: N scale people, animals, automobiles, trucks, signs, signals, junk, and litter. A wide selection of N scale figures, vehicles, signs, and other details is available. Do not skimp when adding details to your layout. Remember to place them not only in prominent places but in some out-of-the-way places as well.

Fig. 10-1. Dave Lull took this photograph on the N scale switching layout Bill and Wayne Reid built for a local model railroading meet. Ellsworth Electric was kitbashed.

Buildings – models that don't roll

The first N scale kit you assemble probably will be for a plastic structure, because most other N scale equipment is purchased already built. If you enjoy structure kit assembly, you may want to try structure painting or modifying. Eventually you may build some structures from scratch. See fig. 10-1.

For several reasons structures are a good item on which to learn basic modeling skills: They are a familiar feature of everyday life; they are large enough, even in N scale, to be worked on easily; and they are less expensive per square inch of working surface than rolling stock or motive power.

A wide selection of ready-built structures is also available. Some structures can be purchased in either kit or assembled form. So if kit assembly and modification do not appeal to you, you can still build an attractive model railroad using ready-built structures.

Types of structures

Many types of structures are appropriate for inclusion in a model railroad.

A model of any structure ever built in the U. S. that existed in the time period you are modeling can be added logically to your layout. But the space available on a model railroad is limited, so be selective when choosing structures. We can divide model railroad structures into three classes. In order of importance they are right-of-way structures, trackside structures, and non-railroad structures.

Right-of-way structures are an integral part of the railroad and include bridges, trestles, tunnel portals, snowsheds, turntables, and signals. Many of these items are available in N scale. Include some of these structures to give your railroad an authentic appearance. If you wish to build your own, many plans have been published in the model railroad press. Plans published in larger scales can be inexpensively reduced to N scale on photocopiers. For example, set the copier to 52.5 percent to reduce an HO scale drawing to N. Most drawings published in model railroad magazines include a notice granting permission to

readers to make such copies for their own use.

Trackside structures are as important as right-of-way structures. A railroad's function is to move goods and people from place to place. Each origin and destination point must have a trackside structure for sheltering people and protecting goods. These structures are either railroad-owned or customer-owned. Railroad-owned structures include facilities for transferring goods from ship and truck to train, freight-loading platforms, passenger stations, commuter shelters, freight stations, and servicing facilities for railroad equipment. The customer-owned structures include all industries with a railroad siding. Many trackside structures are available, but if you want to build some of your own from plans, refer to MODEL RAILROADER Magazine.

Non-railroad structures are not as important as the other types, but some should be included on the layout to create a realistic appearance. Include at least a sampling of the structures

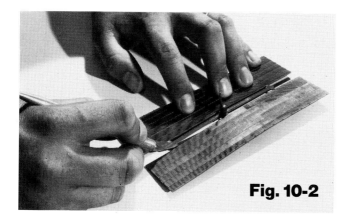

Fig. 10-2

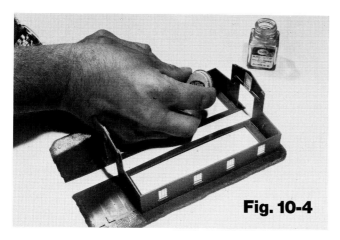

Fig. 10-4

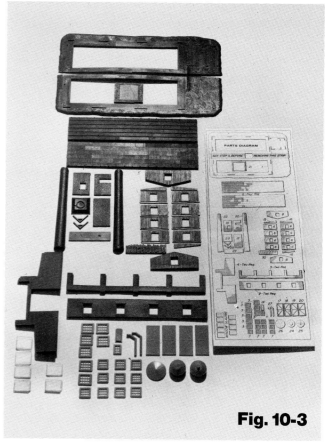

Fig. 10-3

found in a real scene, such as homes, schools, churches, service stations, and factories. While space limitations prevent the inclusion of enough structures to build an exact model of even a small town in N scale, we can create the flavor of a town or city by choosing representative structures.

Structure kit assembly

Plastic kits are easy to assemble. However, time and patience are essential. Plunging ahead to complete the assembly may lead to a ruined model. Follow these suggestions to ensure a satisfactory plastic kit assembly:

• Cut, don't break, all parts from their sprues. See fig. 10-2. Sprues are the lengths of plastic to which kit parts may be attached. (The sprue is the feeder hole through which in manufacturing the plastic is pumped to reach the casting cavities.)

• Spread out all the pieces on a large board, grouping similar pieces together. If the kit instruction sheet contains an illustrated parts list, arrange the parts to coincide with the list. See fig. 10-3.

• Study the instruction sheet. Some instruction sheets are complete, but others may consist only of a drawing.

• Study the relationship of the various parts. Perform some trial assemblies to be certain you know how the model fits together. In some kits each piece has letters imprinted on its inside edge as an assembly guide. The letters on mating pieces should coincide.

• Apply a suitable plastic cement to the inside edges to form joints as shown in fig. 10-4. There are several brands of plastic cement on the market; check their labels to see which is most appropriate for the work you are doing. I frequently use Plastruct Plastic Weld and Testor's Plastic Cement.

Wood kits generally are more difficult to assemble than plastic kits because they require more patience. In addition, the quality of the kit and the completeness of the instructions determine whether a particular kit is easy or difficult to assemble.

Most of the suggestions for plastic kit

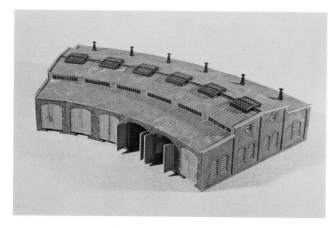

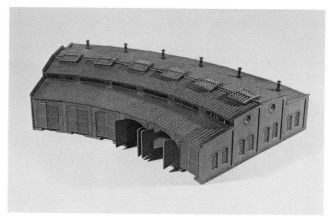

All photos this page, MODEL RAILROADER: A. L. Schmidt.

Fig. 10-5. Plastic structures can be improved by painting them in realistic colors. Here's the Con-Cor roundhouse in its original colors (left) and after repainting in black and brick red (right).

Fig. 10-6. Railroad structures such as this watchman's tower which guarded a Milwaukee crossing are good subjects for a model.

assembly also apply to wood kits. Experiment with different adhesives to find one that works best for you. I usually use Ambroid cement. Other quality brands work well too. Small clamps and a small square are essential for holding parts in correct alignment while the glue is drying.

Painting structures

Plastic structures — The appearance of many commercially painted plastic structures suffers because of unrealistic color schemes. The problem can be remedied by repainting your structures with more realistic colors and color combinations. Let the prototype be your guide. With a little practice you can do a good paint job using small artist-quality brushes.

The difference in appearance of a structure before and after painting can be striking, as illustrated in fig. 10-5. I used Floquil paints on the Con-Cor roundhouse. The Floquil line of paints includes standard railroad colors. This brand of paint goes on nicely with a brush, but it does have one minor drawback: It is a lacquer-base paint and therefore it may soften some plastics. To prevent this from happening, Floquil recommends its primer for plastics called "Barrier."

Floquil's Polly S line of water-soluble paints, which includes standard railroad colors, can be applied directly to plastics. Both Floquil and Polly S paints are available at most hobby shops. Experiment with these and other brands to see which paint best suits your needs.

Wood structures — Finishing instructions usually are included with wood kits. Wood structures can be stained or painted. Generally the instructions advise you to stain the individual pieces before assembly because stain will not "take" on areas where glue has been smeared. Floquil paints also work well on wood.

Kit conversions

You can look at a structure kit two ways. From one point of view, it contains everything you need to build the model pictured on the box. From the other, it is a useful collection of doors, windows, chimneys, roof material, and so on. You can build the model straight from the box, or use your imagination and create a new building.

Why create a new building? To use a hypothetical example, the Brand X farmhouse kit is good as it is. You have one on your layout right now. So does every other N-gauger in your neighborhood, though, and Brand X has just introduced an HO version of the same structure. For the sake of individuality, you could do something different with the Brand X farmhouse.

You could paint it a different color. You could close in the porch to add another room. Or you could buy a second kit and splice the sides together to make a larger house. All it takes is a knife, razor saw, files, plastic cement, courage to make that first cut, and a bit of imagination.

Your imagination requires training. Start by taking a walk through your neighborhood with a notebook and a camera. Notice how one house differs from another in details like doors, windows, shutters, construction material, and basic shape. Notice, too, how some of the houses have more character than others, and try to determine what gives a building character. Record these details in your notebook and on film. Do the same in a business district and around your local railroad. (If you feel

diffident about photographing the grocery store, make mental notes and jot them down when you get home. Be cautious about trespassing on railroad property. Much of your observation can be done from adjacent streets and overpasses.)

As you assemble a few structure kits, you may notice that a handcar shed has windows just like the Brand X farmhouse or that the sides of a warehouse look like the sides in the XYZ roundhouse kit. On your next trip to the hobby shop, look for a kit that could provide the sides and ends for the handcar shed or doors and windows for the warehouse. You probably will not find exactly what you are looking for, but you may find parts and materials for making a structure similar to the handcar shed or the warehouse.

You will discover a wide variety of parts if you look at the kits as collections of pieces. They are well made, accurately scaled, and not expensive, particularly if you consider the time and effort needed to scratchbuild a window or a door in N scale.

Let's take an example of training the imagination. Figure 10-6 shows photographs of a crossing watchman's tower. The tower looks "railroady" and has character. It also looks complex, with its eight sides, pointed roof, open stairway, and little details such as the bell, the chimneys, and the coal bin. Like any building, though, it is made up of individual components. Are any of those components available in kits? Inspect a catalog or the kit boxes in the hobby shop. Windows and doors of the right size and appearance should be easy to find. The stairs and the coal bin might require more searching. The eight-sided pointed roof will be difficult to find, but you could easily scratchbuild

Fig. 10-7. John Morton's kitbashed enginehouse with the roof removed.

John Morton.

Fig. 10-8. John Morton wanted a car and locomotive shop for his Morham & Oro Valley Railroad. The type of structure he had in mind was not available commercially, so he created one of his own design using three Pola Old Railway Repair Building kits, some Plastruct structural shapes, and miscellaneous other plastic parts.

that part of the tower from eight small triangles of cardstock, using strips of tissue to simulate roofing paper. You could slice the sides from a kit for a wood house or use some sheet styrene scribed to simulate the clapboard sheathing.

A model kitbashed or cobbled up in this manner probably will not match the prototype inch for inch. Just try to maintain reasonable dimensions. (Stand up and reach above you. How high is the ceiling? How wide is a door? Take a few basic measurements at home and at work to get an idea of the dimensions common in residential and commercial buildings.) If in addition you can capture some of the character of the prototype in the details of construction and the finish, you can create a convincing representation of the prototype.

After several kit conversions, you will accumulate odds and ends of leftover material. Don't throw them away. From time to time rummage through the scrap box. A few spare parts can form the nucleus of a structure. Instead of finding parts to build a model of a specific prototype, you will find yourself hunting through your photographs and notes for a prototype to match the parts you have. It's all part of the fun of model railroading.

Examples of kit conversions

John Morton needed a car and locomotive shop for his Morham & Oro Valley Railroad. The building he imagined was not available commercially. However, he discovered several items that looked promising while examining kits at the hobby shop.

One that he found was a Pola kit with sides resembling modern brick-and-glass construction. The kit (three of them) became the nucleus of the structure.

Other items included Plastruct girder, angle, and channel shapes for the frame-

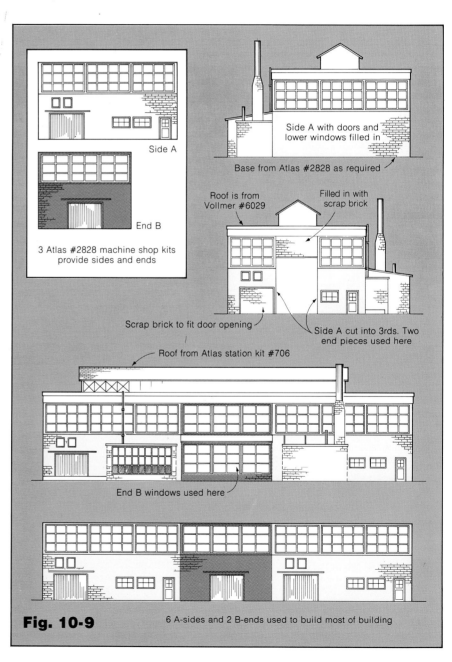

Side A

End B

3 Atlas #2828 machine shop kits provide sides and ends

Side A with doors and lower windows filled in

Base from Atlas #2828 as required

Roof is from Vollmer #6029

Filled in with scrap brick

Scrap brick to fit door opening

Side A cut into 3rds. Two end pieces used here

Roof from Atlas station kit #706

End B windows used here

Fig. 10-9   6 A-sides and 2 B-ends used to build most of building

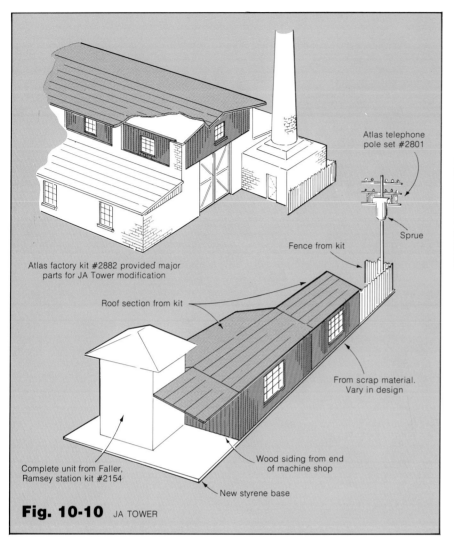

Atlas factory kit #2882 provided major
parts for JA Tower modification

Roof section from kit

Fence from kit

Atlas telephone
pole set #2801

Sprue

From scrap material.
Vary in design

Complete unit from Faller,
Ramsey station kit #2154

Wood siding from end
of machine shop

New styrene base

Fig. 10-10 JA TOWER

John Morton.

**Fig. 10-12. Morton built this shed with
scrap parts from plastic kits.**

work of the building, fence to be used for
catwalk, stairs from an Atlas overpass,
Vollmer roof material, and a section of
platform canopy from an Atlas kit. In
addition, Morton's scrap box yielded
bits and pieces of material.

The photographs, figs. 10-7 and 10-8,
and the drawings shown in fig. 10-9 illustrate Morton's construction method
and the result. The drawings were
made after the building was completed
rather than before. Similar to many
kitbashers, Morton forms a mental im-
age of the structure and works directly
with the materials.

The signal tower of figs. 10-10 and
10-11 was a similar project. It began
with a Faller kit; Morton added a small
shed and various details using materials left over from an Atlas factory kit.

The locomotive shop and the signal
tower both were started with a definite
idea of the finished structure in mind.
The maintenance-of-way shed, fig. 10-
12, on the other hand, began as an
empty place on the layout that needed
a structure. While looking through his
scrap box, Morton found pieces of a
Pola factory kit and realized that a
shed could be built from them — a perfect space filler for the vacant spot by
the tunnel portal. Construction took
only a few hours including such details
as the rail racks and the lengths of rail.

These structure conversions took care
and patience both in construction and in
finishing. All parts had to fit squarely,
and the colors and textures had to
blend realistically. In addition, each
model had to be settled into the layout,
instead of being placed on top of the
scenery at random. Because of these ef-
forts, the models looked like part of the
final setting.

But the biggest satisfaction from kit
conversion comes when a friend ad-
mires your handiwork and asks "Where
do you buy your kits? I've never seen
that one."

John Morton.

**Fig. 10-11. This signal tower is another example of Morton's kit-conversion abilities.
The tower itself was built from a Faller kit. The shed and other details were added
using materials left over from a Pola factory kit.**

Fig. 11-1. The E, Z & Kwick Railroad (it's really a door in disguise!) will teach you the fundamentals of N scale model railroading.

The E, Z & Kwick – a first railroad

The E, Z & Kwick Railroad is an ideal beginner's layout. Almost no carpentry work is required because the layout is built on an inexpensive interior door. Track laying is easy because sectional track is used. There is no complicated wiring to be done; connect two wires and you are ready to operate.

Because of its simplicity, anyone can build this attractive layout.

Even if you feel you are ready to start in N scale model railroading by building a more complex layout, I would caution against it. Construction of a small layout will teach you a lot about each phase of the hobby in a

short time. With this experience, you'll be better prepared to successfully design and build that dream empire. This plan was adapted from plan 62 in the book *N Scale Model Railroad Track Plans* published by Kalmbach. Many other excellent plans for beginners can be found in that soft-cover book.

BILL OF MATERIALS

Item	Description
Interior door	2'-6" x 6'-0" (or larger). An inexpensive Masonite door filled with Styrofoam is ideal.
Paint	1 pint of dark green or brown.
Track (Rapido)	2 pr. manual switches, 9 pcs. 9" straight track, 5 pcs. 4½" straight track, 4 pcs. 2¼" straight track, 5 pcs. 17"R 15° curved track, 11 pcs. 9" R 45° curved track, 2 track clips.
Roadbed	2 pkgs. Atlas cork roadbed.
Power pack	Any pack designed for N scale.
Ballast	1 pkg. N scale ballast. I used a red color from John's Lab.
Plaster	20 pounds of Hydrocal plaster, molding plaster, or Plaster of Paris. Any of them will do.
Dry colors or temperas	At least these three: green, yellow, and burnt sienna.
Rit dyes	Cardinal red, yellow, and black.
Paper towels	1 package or 1 roll.
Styrene	2 square feet, .020" thick.
Adhesives	1 pint of white glue, 1 tube of Ambroid cement, 1 bottle of plastic cement, and 1 8-oz. bottle of acrylic polymer medium (necessary only if you use it for bonding the ballast).
Structures	See table below.
Locomotives	Any switching locomotive.
Rolling stock	Any rolling stock except jumbo freight cars.

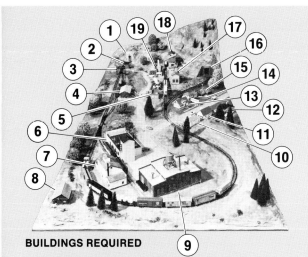

BUILDINGS REQUIRED

1. Tunnel portal — Alexander scale models.
2. Interlocking tower — Bachmann No. 7103.
3. Signal bridge — Bachmann No. 7003.
4. Freight station — Heljan (Con-Cor) No. 641.
5. Auto body repair shop — Bachmann No. 7208.
6. Cold storage building — Heljan (Con-Cor) No. 674.
7. Grain mill — Heljan (Con-Cor) No. 670.
8. Barn — Bachmann No. 7201.
9. Steel-supply warehouse — Heljan (Con-Cor).
10. Gas station — Bachmann No. 7101.
11. Bungalow — Heljan (Con-Cor).
12. Contemporary house — Bachmann No. 7303.
13. Modern house — Heljan (Con-Cor).
14. Split-level house — Bachmann No. 7203.
15. House under construction — Atlas No. 2827.
16. Timber tunnel portal — Campbell Scale Models.
17. Warehouse — Pola No.239.
18. Gravel tower — Model Power No. 1518.
19. Large factory — Vollmer No. 7900.

Fig. 11-2. First, gather the items specified in the Bill of Materials. Most supplies can be obtained at a well-stocked hobby shop, but you will also have to shop at a hardware store, a lumberyard, a dimestore, and an art supply house.

Fig. 11-3. Painting the door serves two purposes: (1) It prevents the door from warping when the wet plaster is applied to it during scenery construction, and (2) by using a dark green or brown paint, it makes areas not covered by plaster look like grass or dirt.

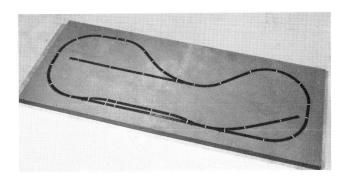

Fig. 11-4. Assemble the track and position it on the door as shown. See the Bill of Materials.

Fig. 11-5. Hold the track in position and outline the track plan on the door by tracing along the ends of the ties.

Fig. 11-6. After tracing, remove the track. The outline of the track route provides a guide for laying cork roadbed.

Fig. 11-7. Atlas cork roadbed has a partial bevel cut down its center, and the two pieces split apart easily.

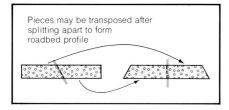

Pieces may be transposed after splitting apart to form roadbed profile

Fig. 11-8. As shown in the drawing above, the two halves of the Atlas cork strip can be transposed to form a realistic bevel-edged track roadbed.

Fig. 11-9. The cork is flexible and can easily be shaped to conform to the track plan drawn on the door. Fasten the roadbed to the door using small wire nails and white glue. Trim the cork with an X-acto knife or single-edge razor blade.

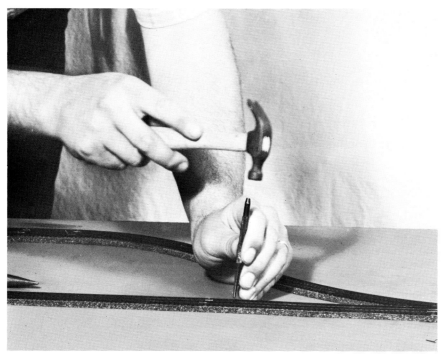

Fig. 11-10. Assemble the track on top of the cork roadbed and fasten it to the road-bed using small wire nails. Holes are provided in the center of the ties for the nails. Gently tap the nail until its head rests on top of the tie. Don't try to drive it in too far or the tie will be bent, distorting the track. A square-end punch or nail set works well for the final hammer blows. Note in fig. 11-17 that two wires must be attached to the track. It is necessary to cut a groove in the cork roadbed for the wire that is attached to the inner rail, or it will cause a hump in the track.

Fig. 11-11. (Top) After the track has been securely fastened to the roadbed, add the ballast. Begin by applying it between the rails; a paper cut makes a good dispenser. Use your little finger to spread the ballast evenly to tie-top height (fig. 11-12, above. Don't apply ballast between the rails of the Rapido switches; ballast particles will foul switch movement.

Fig. 11-13. Next apply ballast to roadbed shoulders using a piece of cardstock or styrene held against the bottom edge of the roadbed as a form. When the form is removed, the ballast will spread to form a sloping shoulder.

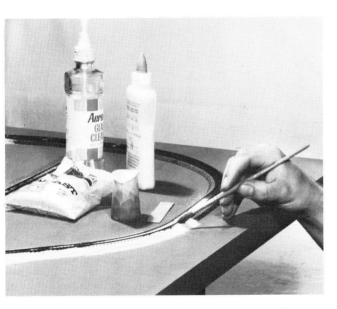

Fig. 11-14. Minor irregularities in the shape of the ballast can be corrected with a small artist's brush.

Fig. 11-15. Next, bond the ballast to the roadbed. Wet the ballast, using a window-type sprayer, with a solution of water and a few drops of detergent. The detergent makes the water "wetter," permitting the bonding agent to spread evenly.

Fig. 11-16. Applying bonding agent to the wet ballast. A bonding agent of diluted polymer medium (dilute 1:1 with water) or diluted white glue (4 parts water to 1 part white glue) can be used. I used an old white-glue bottle as a bonding agent dispenser, but an eyedropper actually works better.

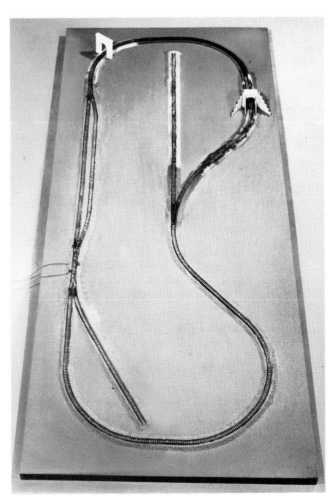

Fig. 11-17. This is how the layout looks with the track ballasting completed and the tunnel portals installed. Concrete tunnel portals would be more appropriate for a contemporary layout such as this one, but I couldn't resist using a Campbell timber tunnel portal.

Fig. 11-18. Before starting scenery construction, assemble all the structures you plan to use on the layout and place them in position on the train board to obtain a general idea of what the finished layout will look like. At this stage of construction, I took some time out to operate trains. Notice that all manual switches will be within easy reach of the power pack!

Fig. 11-19. The only carpentry work necessary for this layout is the cutting of the Masonite pieces which serve as scenery formers at the end of the layout where the tunnel is located. See fig. 11-18. Fasten the scenery formers to the doors with finishing nails and white glue. For the tunnel enclosure I used .020″ styrene; cardboard would warp when the wet newspaper and plaster were added. Note that the track has been covered with masking tape. Do this before beginning scenery construction.

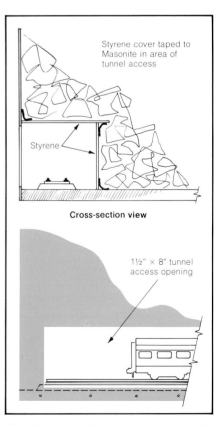

Styrene cover taped to Masonite in area of tunnel access

Styrene

Cross-section view

1½″ × 8″ tunnel access opening

Fig. 11-20. Place wads of crumpled newspaper around the tunnel enclosure to serve as a form for the hard-shell scenery. Using a window-type sprayer, thoroughly wet the newspaper before applying the plaster.

Fig. 11-21. Derailments in a tunnel can be frustrating. Provide some sort of access to the tunnel on your layout. A small slot cut in the scenery former will allow you to extract derailed cars.

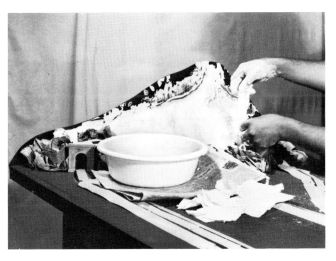

Fig. 11-22. Mix a small batch of plaster (an amount you can use in 5 minutes) to the consistency of pancake batter. Remember to add the plaster to the water.

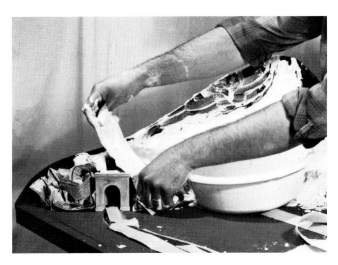

Fig. 11-23. Tear paper towels into 2″-wide strips and squish them around in the plaster until they are thoroughly saturated. Drape the plaster-soaked towels over the wet newspaper.

Fig. 11-24. This initial shell of plaster will look rough, so apply a finish coat of plaster with a wide paintbrush to smooth the appearance of the terrain. Incidentally, a few good raps with the hammer will crush and remove the hardened plaster from the brush. Still another plaster coat can be added if you wish to carve in rock details.

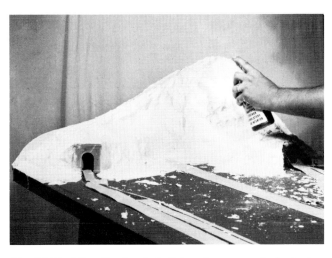

Fig. 11-25. After the hard-shell terrain comes zip texturing. First color any areas not to be covered by the dry pigments. Use various shades of diluted dyes and apply them with eye-droppers or brushes. Next, wet the plaster in areas where you will apply dry pigment. Many modelers add a little black dye to the water to dye plaster as it is being wetted.

Fig. 11-26. Sift on dry colors with a sieve. Sift on brown first to represent ground, and then green to represent grass. The final result is quite dramatic. Most areas are green, but in some places the brown "earth" shows through.

Fig. 11-27. After the major portion of the scenery has been completed, remove the masking tape protecting the track. Plaster adjoining the tape will crumble. A vacuum cleaner will clean up this mess.

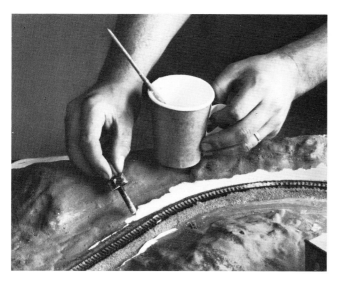

Fig. 11-28. Some plaster touch-up may be necessary after the tape has been removed. A small brush and an eyedropper are the best tools for this work.

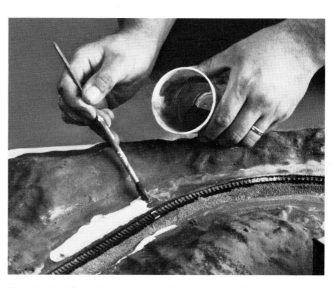

Fig. 11-29. After this touch-up plaster sets, color it with dye to match the surrounding terrain. Brush on brown color with an artist's brush.

Fig. 11-30. Sift on the green pigment over the touched-up area to match the texture of the adjoining terrain.

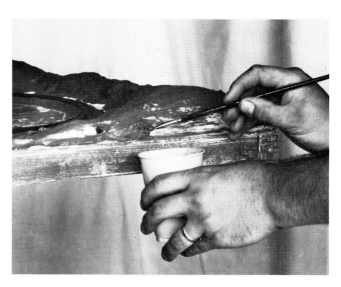

Fig. 11-31. Special effects can be created on rock faces by applying various colors and dyes with a small brush.

Fig. 11-32. An eyedropper filled with dye also can be used to create natural-looking erosion effects.

Fig. 11-33. Two measurements are important when placing trackside structures: height above the rail and distance from the track. To correctly position a structure, put a box car on the track and shim up the structure until its loading ramp is even with the bottom of the box car door. The structure should be at least ⅝″ from the center of the track.

Fig. 11-34. Cut cardstock or Strathmore board to fit the base of the structure and then glue the structure to the layout board (door) using white glue or Ambroid cement.

Fig. 11-35. After the structures have been glued in place, bring the terrain up to the structure foundations by carefully troweling plaster around them.

Fig. 11-36. Smooth the plaster over the area adjacent to the building. Remove excess plaster before it hardens.

Fig. 11-37. Zip texture the new terrain around the structures. Again, use a small funnel to direct the dry colors.

Fig. 11-38. I used .020″ styrene for roads and sidewalks. Thin styrene is durable, yet easy to cut and shape.

Fig. 11-39. Attach styrene to layout with white glue or Ambroid cement. Paint styrene light gray to resemble concrete.

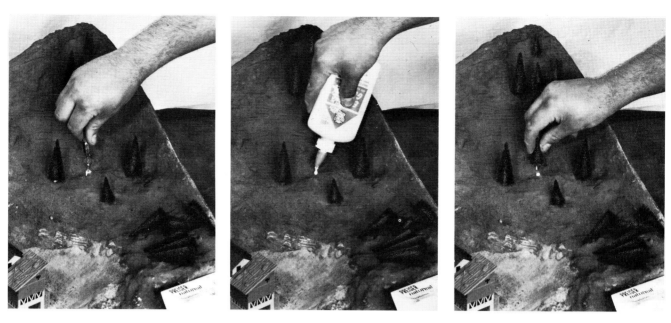

Fig. 11-40. To "plant" a tree drill a hole in the plaster (left). Squirt glue or cement in the hole and on the base of the tree (center) and insert tree (right). Touch up the terrain.

Fig. 11-41. Details make a layout interesting, so don't forget to add such items as figures, cars, trucks, packages and litter.

Fig. 11-42. Other details should include parking lots, roads, and driveways for the industries your railroad will serve.

Fig. 11-43. This gravel quarry and gravel tower on the author's E, Z, & Kwick Railroad even has conveyor buckets and hoppers loaded with N scale gravel.

Fig. 11-44. After the layout is detailed to your satisfaction, clean the rails thoroughly, stage a "last spike" ceremony, and begin operating your railroad!

How many times have you said to yourself when paying a repair bill, "I could have done it myself if only I had had the proper tools for the job"? Proper tools also are important in model railroading. You may have some small tools on hand that are suitable; if so, all the better. However, trying to get along with misfit tools will discourage your interest in the hobby quicker than anything else.

When shopping for tools, don't shop for price alone. Quality tools cost a little more initially, but over the years they will prove to be better buys. If properly cared for, most quality tools will last a lifetime. Quality is especially important when selecting cutting tools.

A basic tool list

I recommend that a beginning N scaler purchase the tools shown in fig. 12-2 right away. With these tools you can perform simple maintenance and repair work on your locomotives and rolling stock, and you can assemble and paint plastic kits. I did not include the woodworking tools necessary to build benchwork here. A list of recommended woodworking tools is included in Chapter 3. Woodworking tools are needed only occasionally, so you may want to borrow or rent them.

Jeweler's screwdriver set — You will need small screwdrivers for disassembly and maintenance of most locomotives. When using a screwdriver, select one with a blade as wide as the screwhead. Wrong-size screwdrivers or blades with rounded edges are likely to break or mangle screws or mar the surface of the model.

Tweezers enable you to pick up and manipulate pieces too small to handle with your fingers. Buy tweezers with

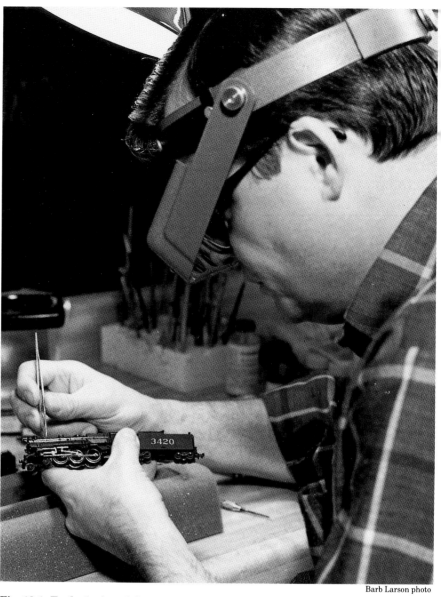

Barb Larson photo

Fig. 12-1. Tools designed for delicate work are needed for maintenance of N scale equipment. A magnifier, as shown above, makes the task easier.

The tools you need

sharp points, or else grind the points so they can be used to pick up small parts easily.

Modeler's knives, such as those made by X-acto, can be used for numerous cutting operations. (A single-edged razor blade is also handy.) Their most common use in N scale is for separating plastic-kit parts from sprues. Only occasionally is it necessary to press hard with a modeler's knife; it cuts just

about as fast with light pressure. The light cut will be more accurate than a heavy one. The blades are razor-sharp, so be careful. A small sharpening stone is useful for keeping the knives in good condition.

Needle files are also called jeweler's files, and they come in many shapes and lengths. Advanced modelers buy them in sets. Probably the two most useful shapes are flat and round, in

lengths of about 5". Use the files for cleaning flash and removing material for a better fit between parts.

Chain-nose pliers have a variety of uses: positioning small parts, wrapping wire around terminals, bending wire to form small parts, holding small parts while working on them, and getting into hard-to-reach places. They are the most useful kind of pliers. Do not use this type of pliers to tighten nuts or for

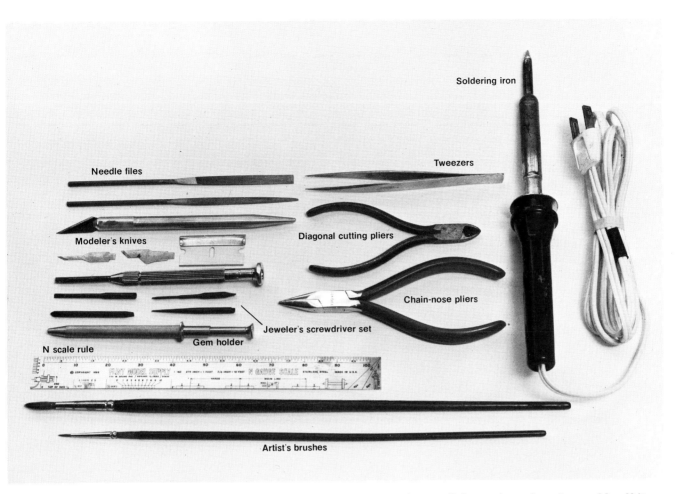

Fig. 12-2. A basic set of tools that can be used for maintenance of N scale equipment, light repair work, and assembly of kits.

any other operation that twists the jaws sideways.

Diagonal-cutting pliers — These can be used for cutting wire, small nails, screws, and even the ends of small shapes of stripwood for a rough cut before dressing with a file. Do not use them on music wire or other springy steel. This tool will receive lots of use, so buy one of good quality initially.

Gem holder — This tiny tool is used by jewelers for handling gems. It is also useful for handling small N scale parts. When the top plunger of the tool is depressed, three steel claws emerge from the bottom of the tool. These claws pick up and hold small parts such as screws and nuts during assembly work.

N scale rule — You can assemble plastic kits without a scale rule but a scale rule would be a wise purchase. With the rule you can compare model and prototype dimensions, for instance. You will also be in a better position to improvise alterations and additions to plastic kits.

Artist's brushes — With a high-quality brush, such as a sable-hair brush, you can paint your models almost as evenly as with an airbrush.

Small soldering iron — A 30- or 40-watt soldering iron is needed for wiring the layout and making electrical repairs to your motive power. A roll of resin-core solder containing about 63

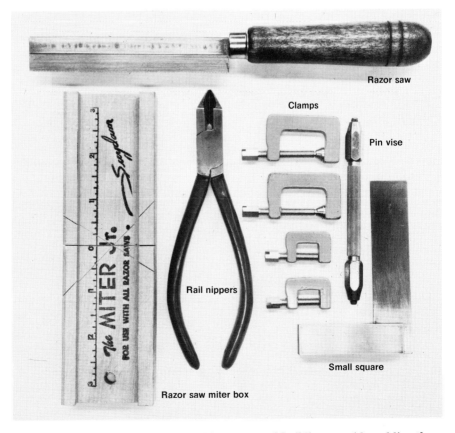

Fig. 12-3. If you should do any kitbashing or scratchbuilding, consider adding these items to your basic tool kit. If you want to lay flexible track, you will need either a razor saw or rail nippers.

percent tin and 37 percent lead (the solder will be marked 63/37) is recommended for soldering electrical connections, but the 60/40 variety is close enough. The resin core is important because the resin is a cleaning agent which removes surface oxides and ensures that the solder will bond to the metal surface. Be sure to take the necessary precautions to prevent fire when working with a soldering iron. Unplug the iron as soon as you are finished.

Other useful tools

After you have been in the hobby awhile you will discover many other useful tools to add to your basic group. Consider these:

Razor saw — The razor saw resembles an old-fashioned straight razor but has teeth on its edge. See fig. 12-3. It has a fine-toothed blade held rigidly in place by a "backbone." A razor saw can cut all materials commonly used in model railroading. It can make fine cuts accurately, and it can cut in places where other types of saws would be awkward. You need either a razor saw or a rail nipper if you plan to use flexible track.

Razor saw miter box — A miter box is a handy angle-cutting guide for your razor saw (fig. 12-3). Several brands are offered at hobby shops with angle-cutting guides available for 90-, 60-, and 45- degree angles.

Rail nippers are heavy-duty diagonal-cutting pliers designed for cutting rail. The pair shown in fig. 12-3 is offered by Lambert Associates.

Clamps of various sizes and shapes, either store-bought or homemade, are a must for assembling wood kits. Use them to hold joined pieces while the glue is drying. Clamps are also handy for holding an item when performing a "three-handed" assembly procedure.

Small square — To do quality work you should have a square to ensure that those 90-degree angles really are 90 degrees. The great temptation is to "eyeball" everything. A square also is a handy jig for forming 90-degree joints: Clamp the pieces to be joined to the square while the glue is drying.

Pin vise — The pin vise is actually a collet with a handle, something like a drill chuck. It is most often used to hold small drill bits when drilling. A pin vise also will hold small taps for threading holes, and you can use it to hold small parts while working on them.

Small vise — A vise can hold parts so you can use both hands to hold a tool. If you buy a vise with metal gripper jaws, be sure to place a piece of wood or other protective material on each side of the part to prevent marring. Several of the small vises sold in hardware and hobby shops are well suited for model railroad work. The vise shown in fig. 12-4 includes a sturdy metal plate for a work surface. Several types of interchange-

Fig. 12-4. The small vises offered by PanaVise, Dremel. General, X-acto and others are well suited to model railroad work. Shown is a PanaVise low-profile jaw vise in a low-profile base mounted to a surface plate.

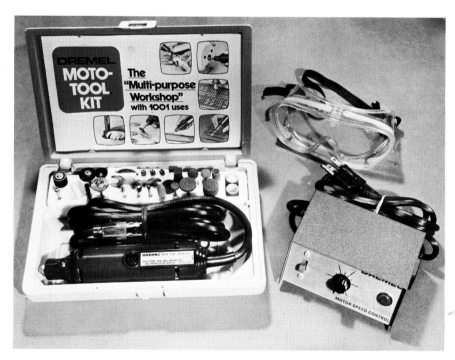

Fig. 12-5. A motor tool is handy for model railroad work. I suggest also buying a speed control; safety glasses are a "must" with a motor tool.

able vise bases, heads, and jaws are offered by PanaVise.

Magnifier — Eventually you may want to consider a magnifier as an aid for modelworking. Many are suitable for model work. I use an Optivisor like the one shown in fig. 12-1. The visor fits over eyeglasses and it can be flipped up when not in use.

Motor tool — A motor tool is handy for model work and can be used to drill, cut, sand, grind, and polish. The Dremel Moto-Tool kit shown in fig. 12-5 comes with a storage case and 34 accessories. You can buy a motor tool with a built in speed control or a separate one. Motor tools run too fast for many model railroad applications on full line voltage. Remember to always wear safety glasses when using a motor tool.

Along the N scale right of way

It's a still morning in the barren high country west of Cheyenne, Wyoming. Then the stillness is broken by a rising whine and rush, and Sherman Hill shakes with the power of 9000 horses as two Union Pacific turbines meet just outside the west portal of Hermosa Tunnel. Jim Kelly built the models and the N scale diorama; Art Schmidt took the photo.

You're overlooking the bustling (or soon to be) mining town of Red Mountain, Colorado, as narrow gauge Denver & Rio Grande K-28 No. 478 rolls into town. Mark Wilson and Keith Koch exercised their modeler's license in putting a K-28 on the Silverton, but when you're working on Nn3 you're allowed a substantial amount of license! Mark and Keith built this prototypically faithful scene, then Mark photographed it and won first prize in MODEL RAILROADER Magazine's seventh annual photo contest.

(Above) Dave Hannah models Southern Pacific's Sacramento Division in his California garage. Here we see a model of SP's beautiful steam-era *Daylight* passenger train pulling into Colfax. Prototype *Daylights* didn't run on this part of the SP, but that's the beauty of model railroading. You can operate YOUR trains anywhere YOU want. (Below) This fabulous ore dock is the work of Dan Cermak of Minnetonka, Minnesota, and is based on the Duluth, Missabe & Iron Range's dock on Lake Superior at Two Harbors, Minn. The chutes are made of Plastruct channel. Parts from HO crossing bridge kits were used for the ore dock's legs. Dan incorporates this and other Ntrak modules into his home model railroad layout.

A. L. Schmidt

Greg Johnson borrowed Sam Lowe's nicely scenicked Ntrak module to use as a setting for this photo of a pair of his own painted and weathered Rock Island F units pulling a branch-line freight.

If you don't think you have space for an N scale layout, how about building it in a piece of furniture? Richard Perrelli constructed his N scale empire into this 2½′ x 4½′ coffee table. It includes a two-lap main line, industrial sidings, a waterfront, operating drawbridge, a yard, an engine facility, and scenery. The controls are located in a drawer, and the layout has working signals. A ⅜″-thick removable plate-glass top protects the railroad. Richard took the photo.

This superb N scale model railroad layout scenery and photograph are the work of Philip Lawson of Springfield, Pennsylvania. The Key Imports Baldwin P5 4-6-2 has just passed Chester Falls and is rounding Snyder's Peak with Chester River far below.

Here's a scene on Pat Lana's Crandic Route, a free-lance line based on Iowa's Cedar Rapids & Iowa City RR. Here at Bennington Yard we get a look at the servicing facilities. The sanding tower, coaling tower, and roundhouse are three of many structures scratchbuilt by Pat.

(Far left) It is Geeps traveling both over and under the bridge on the impressive San Jose Society of Model Railroaders' massive N scale club layout. Construction began on the 20′ x 37′ layout in 1981. The N scale layout is housed in a spacious clubhouse with an HO scale model railroad layout. There are still unfinished areas on the railroad, but what is completed is top-notch. (Left) The track gang in the foreground had to set off their speeder to get out of the way of the long freight with six units of pooled power at the head end. The equipment shown was painted by Tom Harris. Both photos were taken by Malcolm Furlow.

Kent Lannert's module re-creates Railroad Street in Freeburg, Ill. It features all scratchbuilt structures.

Ntrak – another way to enjoy N scale

Ntrak is the N scale version of modular railroading. People participating in this activity generally call themselves Ntrakers. An Ntraker builds a railroad scene on a module that is 2 feet wide and can be either 4, 6, or 8 feet long. And he or she builds it according to common standards so that it can be connected to other modules, including corner modules, to form a layout. If the standards are adhered to, modelers working independently, who have never met one another, can successfully link up their modules at an Ntrak event. If you can get together four corner modules with a few straight ones, you can set up an Ntrak layout and have trains running in a short time. Some huge Ntrak layouts have been assembled at national conventions featuring over 80 modules and measuring 50 x 150 feet.

The reason Ntrak modular railroading works so well is that in 1:160 proportion you can build a pretty extensive scene in a 2 x 4-foot space. You can

build a town scene with some industries for switching, realistic mountain scenery that dominates the trains, or a detailed engine-servicing facility. Some Ntrakers design and build two or three modules with a common theme that can be incorporated into a home club layout when not set up as part of an Ntrak layout.

History

Ben Davis of Huntington Beach, California, came up with the idea and name Ntrak in 1973. Ben was a member of the Belmont Shore Railroad Club in Signal Hill, Calif., and club members helped him build the first modules. The first large Ntrak display was set up at the National Model Railroad Association's (NMRA) 1974 national convention in San Diego. That layout with its prototypically long freight trains of between 50 and 100 cars was an immediate hit. The word spread quickly and soon Ntrak modules were

being built all over the country. Ben Davis volunteered to serve as the coordinator of this effort and started publishing the *Ntrak Newsletter*.

In 1977 Jim FitzGerald took over as coordinator of the Ntrak activities and editor of the newsletter, which has grown to a 48-page bimonthly publication with about 3000 subscribers. If you want to set up a large Ntrak display in your area, Jim is the person to contact because he knows most of the Ntrakers around the country and the type of modules they have built. You'll find his address included in the listing of suppliers and organizations on page 99 of this book.

Visibility

The modular railroading idea started by Ben Davis for N scale quickly spread to the other major scales. Prior to modular railroading, the hobby was an almost invisible one. Your neighbor could be a model railroader and you might not

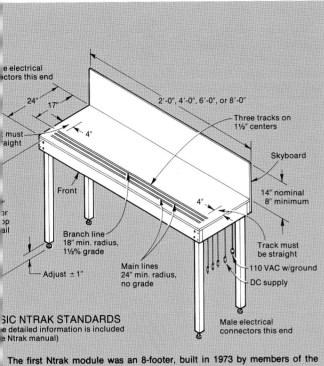

e electrical
ctors this end

24" — 17"

2'-0", 4'-0", 6'-0", or 8'-0"

Three tracks on
1½" centers

must
aight

4"

Front

Skyboard

14" nominal
8" minimum

4"

or
op
ail

Branch line
18" min. radius,
1½% grade

Track must
be straight

Adjust ± 1"

Main lines
24" min. radius,
no grade

110 VAC w/ground

DC supply

Male electrical
connectors this end

SIC NTRAK STANDARDS
e detailed information is included
e Ntrak manual)

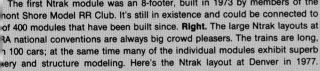

The first Ntrak module was an 8-footer, built in 1973 by members of the
hont Shore Model RR Club. It's still in existence and could be connected to
of 400 modules that have been built since. **Right.** The large Ntrak layouts at
RA national conventions are always big crowd pleasers. The trains are long,
n 100 cars; at the same time many of the individual modules exhibit superb
ery and structure modeling. Here's the Ntrak layout at Denver in 1977.

Jim Hediger photo

even know it unless he or she invited you into that inner sanctum known as *the layout room*. Those people putting on model railroad shows had to be content with sectional layouts designed for such purposes, if they could find some, or small portable layouts.

Modular railroading has greatly increased the visibility of the hobby. Enthusiastic Ntrakers all over the country frequently assemble large operating layouts in shopping malls and for model railroad shows. This grass-roots promotion has done much to increase the popularity of model railroading in general and N scale in particular. N scale is now the second most popular modeling size.

Standards

The basic Ntrak modular standards are given in the drawing on this page, but if you are going to build a module you should buy a copy of the Ntrak manual, which contains more detailed information. Adhering to the standards will assure that your module will suc-cessfully couple up to others when you take it to your first meet.

I also recommend you contact the *Ntrak Newsletter* to see if other Ntrakers live in your area. Once you get your module or modules built, you'll want to try incorporating it into an operating layout, which is, of course, a big part of the enjoyment of Ntrak. If an active Ntrak club isn't in your area, you can try starting one by sending a notice to MODEL RAILROADER Magazine for inclusion in its memberships open listing in Club News. You could also ask about posting a notice at your local hobby shop that you're interested in starting an Ntrak club.

Advantages

For a newcomer, a big advantage of building an Ntrak module is that it is a way to get a taste of the different facets of the hobby quickly and inexpensively. Even a highly detailed module can be built in three to four months, whereas a large home layout may take years.

The builder of a module also receives recognition for his or her work. Although few people are going to have the opportunity to see your home layout, the module is regularly taken out where others can see it, enjoy it, and offer their praise.

Many modelers who are primarily interested in one of the larger scales have built an Ntrak module for a change of pace. And for those whose primary interest is an N scale home or club layout, building a module offers them a chance to try something different — scenery from another part of the country or buildings and railroad equipment from an era that wouldn't fit the home or club layout theme.

Ntrak is also a social activity. It's a good way to meet other model railroaders with whom you can share information and ideas.

Ntrak modular railroading is one of many ways to enjoy N scale. Building modules can become your sole hobby activity, or it can be an adjunct to your home or club layout building.

Our Ntrak module of the New York Central's Water Level Route at Breakneak Mountain.

Let's build an Ntrak module

By Dick Christianson

Our goal in building this module was to re-create in miniature an actual scene on the New Central's Water Level Route along the Hudson River in New York state in the glory days of steam. The inspiration for the project came from Charles M. Knoll's book *The Water Level Route* (Rochester Chapter, NRHS, Rochester, New York, 1976). On the cover of the book is a striking low-angle color photograph (similar to the black-and-white photo top left, page 82) of a New York Central steam locomotive pulling a long string of *Pacemaker* boxcars out of a tunnel in the distance. To the left is the Hudson River and to the right are steep, rugged, rock cliffs.

It struck me at that moment that this scene would make a terrific Ntrak module! The captions on the backs of our file photos indicated that the setting was Breakneck Mountain, near Cold Spring, N. Y., on the Hudson River —

the New York Central's famous Water Level Route.

I enlisted the help of Gordon Odegard and we started to work up a track plan (Dick is managing editor of MODEL RAILROADER Magazine and Gordon is an associate editor). We decided to extend the module forward 6" (one of the options allowed by Ntrak). Most of the 6" would be used for the Hudson River. Gordy quickly drew up a full-size sketch of the top of the module on a large sheet of paper and ordered the materials. We were on our way.

Modular framework

It's not my intention to explain step-by-step how to build an Ntrak module; instead, I'm simply going to outline the steps involved. If this project interests you, or if you decide to build a module of your own design, write to Ntrak, c/o Jim FitzGerald, 2424 Alturas Road, Atascadero, CA 93422. You should include a stamped, self-addressed envelope and ask for the current price for

the 16-page manual that provides details on modular standards, corner modules, other configurations, wiring, and a basic bill of materials.

We started out by cutting the plywood, remembering, of course, that our module extends 6" further forward than most.

Next we laid the full-size track plan on the plywood and marked where the river was to go. Then we cut out the riverbed and the front 1 x 4 (½" deep) to match. See fig. 14-1.

The next step was to cut and assemble the framing (without the two cross pieces). All framework pieces on our module are glued and screwed in place. We matched up the cross pieces with the cut-out plywood and notched them ½" deep. To attach the two side "skyboard" pieces extending above the tabletop, we cut cleats out of 1 x 2s and glued and screwed them in place.

Gordy and I cut the legs to length and installed leveling bolts in the bottoms. We positioned the legs in the cor-

The builders exercised two options allowed by Ntrak: the module is 6′ long instead of the standard 4′, and 6″ was added to the front.

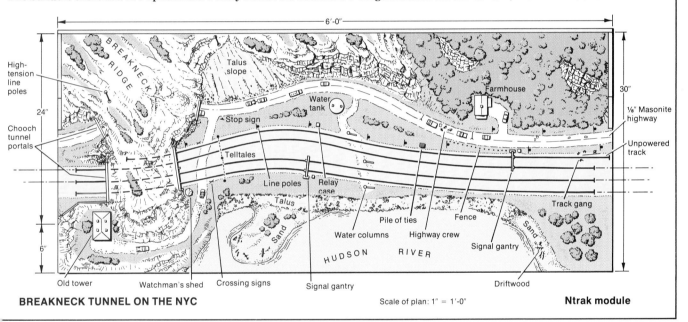

BREAKNECK TUNNEL ON THE NYC

Scale of plan: 1″ = 1′-0″

Ntrak module

ners, clamped them in place with C-clamps, and drilled holes for the bolts. Note in fig. 14-5 that we marked them A, B, C, and D for easy reassembly later.

Track and wiring

We elected to use the new Peco Super N flextrak. With its rails embedded in the ties it looks more realistic than standard Peco track. But, as it turns out, the tops of the new rails are actually about .030″ lower than the standard Atlas track used to join modules. To correct the vertical misalignment, we had to raise the subroadbed about .030″.

The next step was to locate the right-of-way and cement down the .030″ shim. At each end I carefully marked where the track centers were to be, then I laid the track plan over it, lining up the track centers on the tabletop with those on the track plan. Then, with an awl, I punched holes just outside the track-center marks on the track plan. This located the right-of-way for me. Next, I cut out the .030″ shim and cemented it in place (fig. 14-2).

Once again I laid the track plan on the tabletop, lining up the track centers on the table with those on the track plan. Then, again using the awl, I punched holes at roughly 1″ intervals down the center line of each track on the track plan (fig. 14-3). You'll note on the accompanying prototype photos that the Water Level Route (and our module) had four mainline tracks, but Ntrak modules have only three. More on this later when I explain our tunnel arrangement.

The next step was to position the cork roadbed. We placed it so that the inside edge lined up perfectly with the awl holes and were careful to stagger

splices. With the cork strip in position, we tacked it in place. We sliced through the cork at the point where the .030″ cardstock ended and tacked it down (to maintain the .030″ difference). See fig. 14-4.

Once the roadbed was in place, laying track was just a matter of positioning the rails with the roadbed center line directly between the rails and spiking it down. If you use Peco track, you'll need to drill holes in the tie strip for track nails.

For details of wiring, refer to the Ntrak manual. The drawing and photos in fig. 14-5 show how we did it. It's very straightforward. We used only one set of feeders per track, but you could use more if you prefer. You'll note in the photos that Gordy fabricated wooden standoffs and brackets to hold the terminal strips and cords in place. Our module is strictly mainline track, so no

(Above) Our Ntrak module was built to represent this popular railfan spot along the Hudson River north of Cold Spring, New York. The train is a later version of the *20th Century Limited*, powered by 4000-hp EMD E7A and B units. In building the module, the key to capturing the scene was in duplicating the rugged rockwork and the talus pile at the base of the cliffs. Despite the foam base for the mountain, the module is plenty heavy toward the back.

When he took the above photo, the New York Central's photographer was standing just about where MR staff photographer Art Schmidt had his camera positioned for the color photo at right. Through the rock outcropping beneath them passes the New York Central's four-track main line. The above photo and others from MR's files and in books made detailing the scene relatively easy.

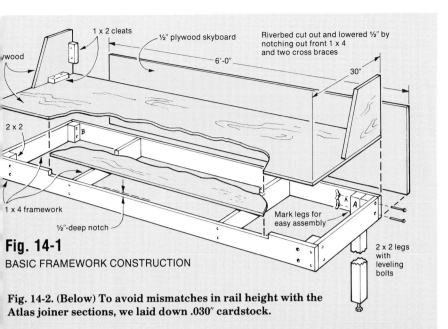

1 x 2 cleats
½" plywood skyboard
Riverbed cut out and lowered ½" by notching out front 1 x 4 and two cross braces
6'-0"
30"
wood
2 x 2
1 x 4 framework
½"-deep notch
Mark legs for easy assembly
2 x 2 legs with leveling bolts

Fig. 14-1
BASIC FRAMEWORK CONSTRUCTION

Fig. 14-2. (Below) To avoid mismatches in rail height with the Atlas joiner sections, we laid down .030″ cardstock.

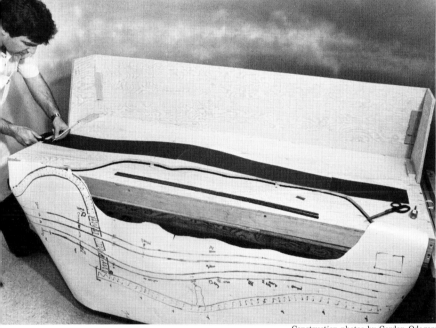

Construction photos by Gordon Odegard

Fig. 14-3. Awl holes made every inch along the track lines on the plan make it easy to position the roadbed.

Fig. 14-4. To make a smooth transition between the module and the joiner sections, an .030″ difference in height was needed. Cement the roadbed to .030″ subroadbed, cut it at the subroadbed, and cement the end pieces directly to the tabletop.

double-pole, double-throw switch is necessary for branchline control. Again, the Ntrak manual goes into the details if your module plan calls for branchline traffic.

Gonna build a mountain

The next step was to build Breakneck Mountain itself. For that I used 2″-thick blue extruded insulating foam. One sheet was all it took. I made a paper template of the bottom piece, traced it on the foam, and cut it. Here's where I have an advantage over most of you. I walked down the hall and cut the foam with an industrial-size bandsaw; most of you won't have that luxury and will need to cut the foam with a serrated knife. It's no fun. I've heard of other modelers who have used a hot-wire device, but watch out for fumes if you do this. Make sure you have plenty of

ventilation. After cutting off the first piece, it was just a matter of cutting the next ones slightly smaller as shown in fig. 14-6.

To cement the pieces together I used Elmer's *water-base* contact cement — the water-base kind does not attack the foam. Once the cement had set up, we used a Surform tool and our serrated knife to shape the mountain. We worked directly from the photos, trying to duplicate the shape as best we could.

The highway running alongside the tracks is ⅛" tempered Masonite cemented directly onto the plywood. The highway tunnel portal is from Chooch.

Before we cemented the top of the hill over the tunnel tracks (you may want to make it removable), we ballasted the tracks and dropped on diluted white glue as shown in fig. 14-7 to bond it in place. When this had finally dried we

airbrushed the ballast a dark gray.

The fig. 14-7 photo also shows the track arrangement inside the tunnel. We modified the too-narrow Chooch portals (cut them apart and spliced pieces in the middle) so that from the south end four tracks go in, but from the north end only three come out. That way we wouldn't have the fourth track abruptly ending at the next module. At the far south end, we removed one section of rail and installed a track gang engaged in work to draw attention away from that dead-end fourth track.

At this juncture Gordy and I just couldn't wait any longer, so we put the water tower, crossing watchman's shed, and power poles on the module, and a model train on the tracks to find out what it was going to look like. See fig. 14-8.

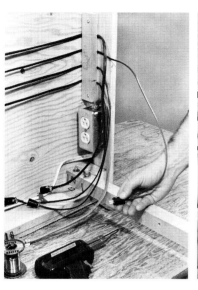
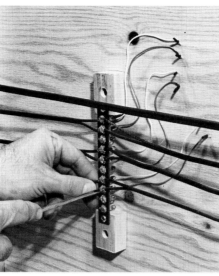
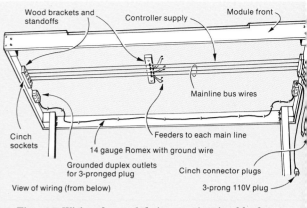

Fig. 14-5. Wiring the module is easy. A pair of feeders to each bus wire is about all there is to it. Cinch connectors at each end make it easy to plug the modules together. The 110V wiring does require care, however.

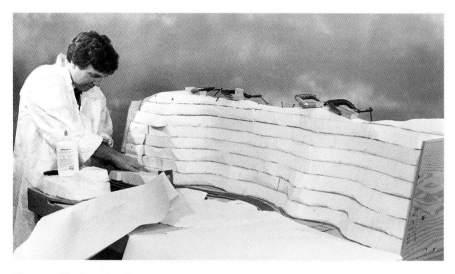

Fig. 14-6. The base for the mountain is cut from 2″-thick extruded blue Styrofoam insulation. Each piece is cut just smaller than the one beneath it to taper it back to the top of the mountain. Use water-based contact cement to glue the sheets together.

Fig. 14-7. Cement the tunnel ballast in place if you intend to transport your module. Use white glue thinned with water and a drop of liquid detergent. The tunnel itself is tricky in that four tracks (the one at left is unpowered) come into it, but only three (Ntrak standards call for three mainline tracks) come out.

Rock castings

The most dramatic part of this module is the rockwork. Since this is the focal point of the scene, it deserved the most attention.

Having done a little rock carving before, I knew that for rockwork this extensive carving was not the way to go; rock molds were the answer. We bought many nice ones from Blue Ribbon Models so that we'd get a variety of rock formations. In retrospect, we could have gotten away with only two or three with bold, dramatic features. Some of the molds we used feature small crevices and outcroppings, really too fine for the massive look of these cliffs.

We weren't really certain how well the plaster would adhere to the Styrofoam mountain, so we pushed galvanized (they don't rust) 20-penny nails into the mountain at various angles (fig. 14-9). We felt like this might give the plaster something to get a grip on.

Then we mixed Hydrocal (a plaster product from U. S. Gypsum) and poured the soupy (about like pancake batter) material into moistened molds. The plaster-filled molds were then slapped (ready when the plaster surface developed little hairline cracks) onto the mountainside. See fig. 14-10.

We quickly learned that tipping the module on its back was the right approach — holding the molds in place in this position was easy on the wrists. We held them in place for several minutes until the plaster had set up well enough for us to peel away the molds without having the plaster crumble.

In positioning the molds we referred to prototype photos to duplicate, roughly, the look of the rocks. The idea was to place a mold where we wanted it and then later, having moistened the first one, to slap down another next to it, partially overlapping the two.

When the plaster had set up pretty well, Gordy and I used screwdrivers (fig. 14-3) to chip away rough edges and stiff-bristle paintbrushes to blend together some molds that didn't look quite right together. We even mixed more Hydrocal, somewhat thicker, and did a little carving in places for a better blend.

Because it's so easy to work with, we used Scupltamold to fill in the gap at the edge of the river where the two layers of plywood met and to build up the sandbar. We thoroughly soaked the plywood first, since dry wood tends to suck the water right out of both plaster and Sculptamold.

Riprap and talus

Not surprisingly, we wasted a few rocks. Either we were too busy or just weren't paying enough attention to notice when plaster had set up in the molds while still sitting on the table. No problem. We smashed these up with a hammer to provide riprap for alongside the river and talus for the base of the cliffs. I used a strainer to separate the pieces: larger for the riprap, smaller for the talus. In fact, the pieces in the talus pile are only one grade above powder.

To apply the talus we again tipped the module back (fig. 14-12) until the hill

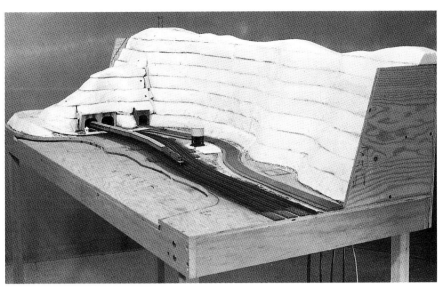

Fig. 14-8. At this point we couldn't wait any longer. We put the water tower, power poles, and crossing guard house on the module and a train on the tracks; then we stepped back and admired our work.

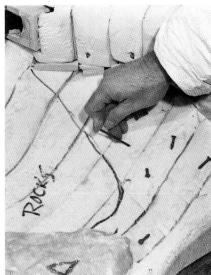

Fig. 14-9. Push 20-penny galvanized nails into the Styrofoam to give the rocks something to grip.

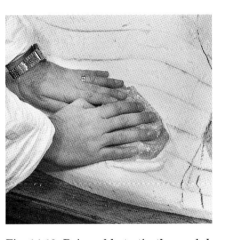

Fig. 14-10. Being able to tip the module over makes holding the rock molds in place less tedious.

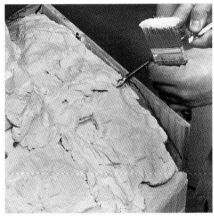

Fig. 14-11. To blend the molds together, chip away at the edges with a screwdriver.

Fig. 14-12. A paper cup came in handy for applying talus. Tipping the module on its back helped again.

was just about parallel to the floor, and then we sprinkled on the talus from a plastic cup. Next, I sprayed on a mist of water-thinned white glue (we also added a couple drops of detergent to make it "wetter") and let it dry overnight before tipping the module back onto its feet.

Fastening the riprap involves roughly the same procedure. I sprinkled the bigger plaster chunks onto the riverbank, letting it take its shape naturally; then I used an eye-dropper to apply water-thinned white glue.

Coloring rocks

MR Associate Editor Jim Kelly does a beautiful job of painting rocks, so I asked if he'd help out. After covering the tracks with tape and other surfaces with paper, Jim painted the rest of the exposed Styrofoam an earth brown latex. This would eventually be covered with lichen. Next, Jim brush painted all of the rockwork with an ordinary water-thinned gray latex paint and let it dry. The next step was to spray the

rock faces with a thin wash of black acrylic paint mixed with water. After letting that dry, he dry-brushed white acrylic on the projections to highlight the rockwork and define its rugged features. See fig. 14-13.

The rocks looked stark and cold. But Jim wasn't done. He dobbed on reds, yellows, and browns. Then he sprayed the rocks with water and let the warm colors run down and work their way into the crevices and onto the flat surfaces. Breakneck Mountain looked great!

I urged Jim to go ahead and paint the rip-rap. Same process, same results. He really is a rock painter extraordinaire!

Jim was encouraged by his success with the rocks and wanted to keep at the job. He used a plastic cup as a dispenser to sprinkle various shades and grades of ground foam onto the layout, adding darker, coarser colors in low areas and near the riverbank. He followed this with a thorough spraying of diluted matte medium to fix the greenery to the surfaces. See fig. 14-14.

Fig. 14-13. Jim Kelly first brush-painted the rocks gray with water-thinned latex paint...

 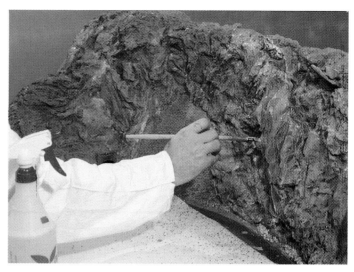

...and then sprayed on thin black acrylic and let it run into the crevices (for shadows). He next brushed on earth tones and sprayed water on the scene and dry-brushed the rocks with white.

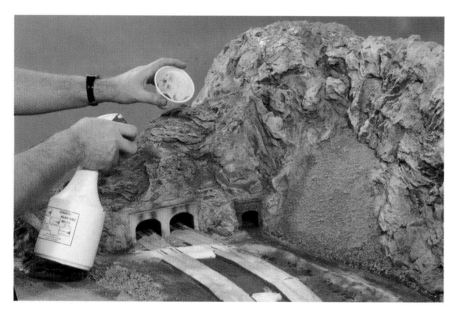

The next step in the greening of the module was to add lichen to the bare end of the mountain. For this step we painted a heavy coating of white glue onto a small part of the mountainside. Then, starting at the bottom, I began sticking clumps of lichen onto the surface (fig. 14-15) while Gordy used a big scissors to cut apart the lichen, giving me only the choice tips of the plants (glued fine tips up). Eventually we had the entire mountainside covered.

Track ballasting

Before ballasting the track, Gordy painted the track. He airbrushed the sides with Floquil Rust and the ties

Fig. 14-14. Sprinkle ground foam, then spray thinned matte medium and the scene looks warm and alive. Add structures and details for the final touches.

Fig. 14-15. Paint a thick coat of white glue onto the Styrofoam and apply the best-looking lichen tips for a lush, forested look.

Fig. 14-16. Shake ballast between and alongside the rails. (Continued at top of next page.)

Color model photos by A. L. Schmidt

A freight train, pulled by brand new F units, races down the four-track main line between the Hudson River and the highway.

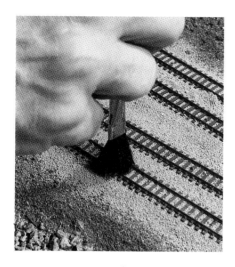  

(Continued from top of previous page.) Then carefully work it into shape with a soft-bristled brush. Next, apply thinned white glue to the ballast; then spray "wet" water on the ballast. Finally, clean the tops of the rails.

with highly thinned Grimy Black. This greatly improves the track's appearance. He cleaned the tops of the rails with a Bright Boy abrasive block before the paint had time to set up hard.

When the paint on the rails had dried, it was time to apply the ballast. Gordy partially filled a plastic cup with ballast, and making a back-and-forth motion with his hand, he worked his way down the tracks. With a soft-bristled brush he next worked his way along the edges of the roadbed to form a good-looking contour and down the middle to get the ballast to fall between the ties and off the rail sides. Gordy followed this with an application of thinned white glue and a thorough soaking with a mixture of water and liquid dish soap (a few drops only). These steps are illustrated in fig. 14-16.

With the ballast permanently in place, Gordy brushed Engine Black highly diluted with Dio-Sol down the middle of the tracks to give them an oily, sooty, greasy, heavily used main-

line look. Just to be safe, he cleaned the rails again.

When all of this had dried, Gordy used a small screwdriver to clean away chunks of ballast stuck to the inside of the rails and an abrasive track cleaner to polish the tops.

The Hudson River

We had mulled over the question of what to do with the river, debating whether to use poured resin or gloss medium. We finally decided that a poured resin surface would add weight, would be subject to a lot of smudge-leaving finger-touching, and might not hold up well to the flexing modules are bound to experience while being transported here and there. We finally settled on gloss medium.

After sanding the plywood smooth and removing all dust and dirt, Gordy sprayed the riverbed with tan paint near the shoreline to simulate shallow water; then he sprayed the rest of it a dark gray to simulate depth. The next step was to paint on gloss medium and then, as it was drying, to stipple it with a brush, lifting it in places to simulate waves (fig. 14-17). The final touch was to highlight the wave tips (give them whitecaps if you will) by applying white paint from an almost dry brush.

Structure and details

At this point the layout looked terrific, but it needed details, most of which are shown in the accompanying photos. Let's work from one end of the module to the other, starting at the southern end.

First, the trees are all made from metal armatures, painted gray, and then Bachmann Poly Fibre was draped over them and ground foam sprinkled onto that. A misting of latex adhesive from a spray can holds the foam in place.

Because of the extra mainline track at this end, Gordy removed one rail and

Fig. 14-17. Stippled gloss medium results in a choppy-looking river.

positioned a track gang hard at work. This activity draws attention away from the track that just ends at the next module.

Behind this crew and up the road a ways is the highway department crew. Gordy gouged a hole in the gray-painted Masonite road, glued in some fine sand, and placed workers around the hole. He built barricades from strip styrene and placed trucks behind them to protect the workers. He's reinforced the idea of roadwork in progress by painting in glossy black tar patches and cracks in the highway. The no-passing stripes in the road are 1/32″-wide decal stripes; the white guard posts are .047″ styrene rod.

Behind the road crew is a house. The prototype for this white frame house shows on a couple of photos we used for reference but were unable to publish; the model is a reasonable representation. Gordy built the house per the kit instructions, painted the roof, weathered it lightly, and dry-brushed it with white to bring out the highlights. He added a number of details, including garbage cans, a dog, and a lady hanging out the wash. He also hung a tire swing from the tree in the yard.

All along the tracks are line poles. These are from Atlas; Gordy painted them dark brown with a blackish base. He painted in the insulators with a silver/green mix. The single high-tension pole on top of the mountain (shows up in many photos) is kitbashed from Atlas single-mast poles.

Across the tracks we placed fishermen, sunbathers on the sandbar, and a rowboat half-filled with water. This neat little detail just barely shows as a dark line in the water on one of our file

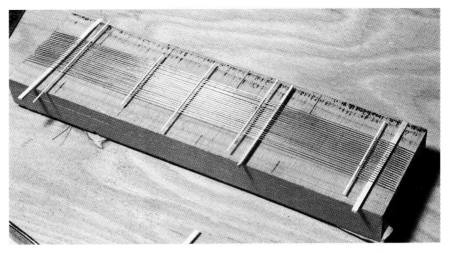

Fig. 14-18. Armature wire stretched tightly over a piece of wood provides the basis for the telltales.

(Above) A pump house sits on the module. A couple of Kibri kits rearranged a bit gave us a reasonable model of the prototype. (Below) One of the many prototype photographs we used to achieve a realistic look to our module.

photos. Driftwood along the riverbank is nothing more than coarse pieces of leftover lichen.

The various signs (i.e., stop, railroad crossing, speed limit, mile marker, and whistle) were made by photostatically reducing dry-transfer designs and then cementing them to styrene.

The distinctive, beautifully lacy signal bridges, the relay cases, and battery boxes were scratchbuilt by Gordy.

Another distinctive trackside detail is the three water columns along the main. These are really nice-looking models from Diamond Scale Construction which were modified a little and painted Floquil Engine Black.

The water tower on the far side of the tracks started out as a kit from Dimi-Trains. The roof was modified and we painted it in a gray and green scheme. We think it's fairly close to prototypical for this period.

The trains

And last, other than vehicles and figures placed here and there, we had to model the trains themselves. We know that the paint scheme on the Hudson is not correct for the 1938 *20th Century Limited*. Gordy did repaint the Con-Cor engine locomotive and tender to match the scheme, but the cars are straight from the box (late 1940s version), though lightly weathered. The *Pacemaker* cars are weathered Kadee models; and the F units are prepainted brass models from Key. They are, of course, of a later vintage.

So that's the story of our Ntrak module.

The *20th Century Limited* races along the Hudson River southbound just north of Cold Spring, New York, on its way to New York City. On the northbound track a *Pacemaker* merchandise freight heads north on its way to Buffalo.

There's UP action aplenty in the Blue Mountains. On the upper line a pair of Trix U28Cs
shove a cut of empty hoppers up to Sargent Coal. Meanwhile, a trio of Con-Cor SD40-2s
drift downgrade towards Pendleton with a long-haul freight train.

The Union Pacific Northern

By Jim Whitehead
Photos by Dave Frary

Mention the Union Pacific RR and
we think of a great, double- and even
triple-track line stretching from the
Missouri River to our Pacific shore. We
think of trains stretching over wind-
swept Sherman Hill, pulled by Big
Boys, Turbines, Centennials, and other
superpower legends.

There is another Union Pacific, how-

ever, one more closely resembling a
Colorado mining railroad. It's a single-
track mountain railroad where 1.1 percent grades are the rule and trains over
4500 tons require mid-train helpers.
This is the Union Pacific's main line
through the Blue Mountains of eastern
Oregon. It's the prototype for my Union
Pacific Northern N scale railroad.

It's 1968 and eastbound UP trains, fol-
lowing the Columbia River up from
Portland, enter my territory just west of
Pendleton, home of the famous Pendle-

ton Woolen Mills. Reith Yard is a busy
place as trains are prepared for the as-
sault on the mountains. After passing
through industrial East Pendleton the
main line struggles uphill until it finally
crests the Blue Mountains in Deadman's
Pass at an elevation of 3796 feet. From
there it descends slowly until it reaches
the division point yards at LaGrande
(elevation 2787 feet) before proceeding
eastward.

My N scale Union Pacific Northern
also includes two branch lines. The Pi-

Two lucky railfans have arrived in Joseph just in time to catch GP9 234 in action. The model is a Hallmark brass import, painted by the author. Robinson Grain is part scratch-built and part kitbashed, and represents the farm industry widespread in eastern Oregon.

The crew of the Pilot Rock local has "gone for beans" after switching the American Potash & Chemical trona refinery at Enterprise. The author scratchbuilt the box-like modern refinery.

lot Rock Branch, source of considerable commodity traffic, winds south from Pendleton. The Joseph Branch heads northward from LaGrande, crosses Mission Hill, and descends to Enterprise on the Wallowa River. The branch then follows the river eastward to reach the rich farmland near Joseph on scenic Lake Wallowa.

Planning the layout

When I first decided to model in N scale I searched through the catalogs and identified those railroads for which the widest range of ready-to-run rolling stock and engines was available. The choices quickly narrowed to the western railroads and the Union Pacific. Then I looked at western railroad

maps and settled on the UP in eastern Oregon because it offered both bridge traffic and two active branches to generate local traffic. Reith is my father-in-law's middle name, so when I learned a Reith Yard was once located near Pendleton, the die was cast.

Having decided upon a prototype, the next step was gathering data. Articles appearing in TRAINS Magazine, *Railroad Model Craftsman*, and MODEL RAILROADER ("A railroad you can model," September 1973) furnished a wealth of information, as did several friends who provided photos from their trips through eastern Oregon. This led to the selection of an era and a list of industries and scenic features to be included on the layout.

Those familiar with eastern Oregon will quickly notice that considerable modeler's license has been exercised to include shippers of petroleum products, petrochemicals, coal, trona, lumber, and grain on the layout. This liberal mixing of fact and fiction also extends to relocating the Northern Pacific from Pendleton to Joseph, Oregon, to generate interchange with more operating possibilities.

The UPN was initially conceived as a one-man home layout; consequently a point-to-loop arrangement was selected. As construction progressed, however, I was introduced to a group of operating enthusiasts and instantly converted to the belief that a layout should be built to operate. After reading up on the subject,

The Blue Eagle Refinery, representing UP subsidiary Champlin Oil, is a major source of traffic on the UPN. The tanks are from a variety of Kibri, Vollmer, and DMK plastic kits.

I quickly realized that the layout under construction had many drawbacks from an operations point of view.

Work was briefly halted while I developed a revised track plan, one that featured point-to-point operation, multiple control stations, and a hidden storage track. This revamped track plan, as shown here, has served well despite compromises made to minimize changes in construction already complete.

The benchwork is a combination of tabletop and L-girder construction with a minimum height above the floor of 36″. Two spirals raise the track to 45″ at its maximum elevation, with an intermediate operating level of 40″ above the floor.

The 36″ height has proved too low, making work under the layout difficult

and the viewing angle somewhat too sharp. The 40″ level is much easier to work under and yet is not difficult to operate. If I were to start again I would set 40″ as my minimum height.

The layout was constructed with an 18″ minimum radius on the main line and a 12″ minimum radius on the branch lines and spurs. I glued the cork roadbed down with white glue, then fastened the track with Pliobond contact adhesive. This combination has shown no deterioration in 6 years of operation.

I used Railcraft's Code 70 flexible track for the main line and its Code 55 for sidings and spurs. Most of the turnouts are Peco, although one or two other brands, mainly Shinohara, have been employed for special applications like

yard ladders and three-way turnouts.

The scenery is rigid polystyrene foam covered with earth-tinted wood putty. I covered this with a layer of Woodland Scenics ground foam soil. After this had dried thoroughly I added accents with various browns and olive green foam, then followed with a light dusting of Turf.

Next I added trees, mixing pines with birch and aspen in the mountain areas. The pine trees are all Woodland Scenics, as I have yet to make a homemade pine I'll permit on my layout. I use bumpy chenille to represent younger pines at the edge of the forest. The birch, aspen, and hardwoods are homemade using a variety of local weeds dipped in ground foam.

Bill Borelli checks the waybills as he prepares to switch a cut of cars just set out at LaGrande.

Jim Whitehead photo

Variety is important to good scenery. I used all sorts of materials: lichen, hemp grass, leftover Woodland Scenics tree foliage, small pinecones, large pieces of ground foam, sand, dirt, small pebbles, and plaster.

One scenic feature that draws a lot of visitor attention is the long cliff across the river from Enterprise. It's there to hide trains so an observer doesn't see trains doubling back in the direction from which they came. It's the kind of trick, as pointed out by John Armstrong in his book *Creative Layout Design* (Kalmbach Publishing Co.), that gives the impression the train is actually going somewhere. It also keeps the uninitiated guessing which tunnel the train will emerge from next.

I created the cliff using Hydrocal plaster in rubber rock molds. Afterwards the cliff was colored with washes of black and blue oil paints to obtain a blue/gray weathered rock effect. Ground foam and lichen were added to represent the weeds and small bushes that inevitably find a toehold on even the steepest cliffs.

Wiring

The UPN is operated by conventional block control with each of the layout's eleven blocks wired to receive power from either of the two mainline cabs. Local control stations permit independent operation of the yards at Reith, LaGrande, and Joseph. We can operate up to five trains at once, two on the main line and three in the yards and their environs.

We use four Power Systems PSI-550 handheld, transistorized throttles and one by Model Rectifier Corp. To avoid voltage drops and surges in train speed, the throttles and switch machines are on separate power supplies. All the wiring is color-coded to simplify troubleshooting and modification.

At present signals are used only to indicate train routing at critical spots and are controlled by switch-machine contacts. Eventually track detection circuitry and block occupancy indication will be added.

Locomotives and cars

Motive power on the UPN is all diesel. Newly arrived six-axle SD40s and U28Cs appear regularly on hotshot scheduled freights like the *Reith Expediter* and the *Overland Mail Express*, while the local freight service is handled by GP7s, GP9s, and some of the few remaining F units.

The three-times-a-week *City of Portland* streamliner normally sports a brace of EMD E8s, but occasionally an A-B-B set of Alco PAs is substituted. Yard switchers are mostly GP7s. These diesels are a mixture of brass and plastic locomotives from a number of different sources, including Atlas, Con-Cor, Hallmark, Minitrix, and Arnold.

The UPN boasts a fleet of 156 freight cars reflecting the types of traffic handled. There are some 36 boxcars, 16 hopper cars, 42 covered hoppers, 19 reefers, 15 tank cars, 8 gondolas or flatcars, and 7 cabeese. All cars are equipped with Kadee couplers and have been weighted, where necessary, to ensure each car weighs more than 1½ ounces.

Operation

Each car has a corresponding car card listing the reporting marks and number and providing a pocket for waybills. A waybill is a simple piece of colored paper with an industry name written on it. Each town on the layout is identified by a specific color, so the yard operator need only block together all cars with waybills the same color, then arrange the blocks in the order specified by a color-coded chart at each station.

Each car card has four waybills. When a car is delivered to the specified industry the top card is moved to the back of the waybill pocket, exposing a new waybill and prompting the next movement.

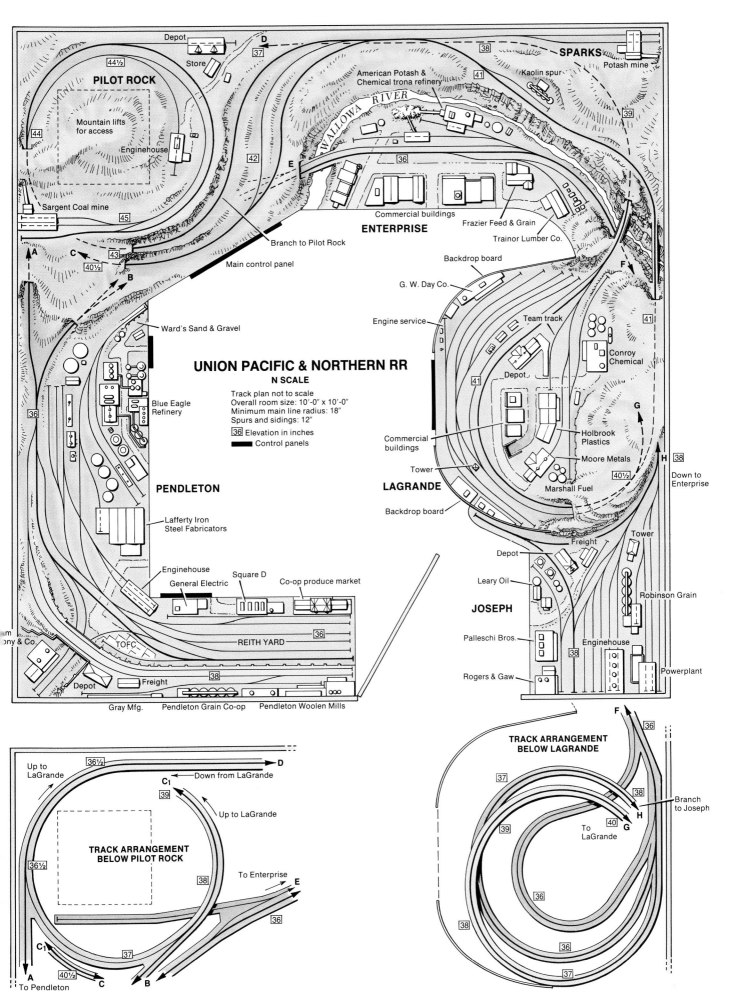

PILOT ROCK

44½

44

Mountain lifts for access

Enginehouse

Sargent Coal mine

45

43

40½

Depot

Store

37

D

Branch to Pilot Rock

Main control panel

42

E

38

41

SPARKS

Potash mine

Kaolin spur

39

41

American Potash & Chemical trona refinery

WALLOWA RIVER

36

Commercial buildings

ENTERPRISE

Frazier Feed & Grain

Trainor Lumber Co.

Backdrop board

G. W. Day Co.

Engine service

F

41

Team track

Conroy Chemical

Depot

41

G

Holbrook Plastics

Moore Metals

H

38

Commercial buildings

Tower

Marshall Fuel

40½

Down to Enterprise

LAGRANDE

Backdrop board

Freight

Tower

Depot

Robinson Grain

JOSEPH

Leary Oil

Palleschi Bros.

Enginehouse

38

Rogers & Gaw

Powerplant

A

C

B

Ward's Sand & Gravel

36

Blue Eagle Refinery

PENDLETON

UNION PACIFIC & NORTHERN RR

N SCALE

Track plan not to scale
Overall room size: 10'-0" x 10'-0"
Minimum main line radius: 18"
Spurs and sidings: 12"

36 Elevation in inches

▬ Control panels

Lafferty Iron Steel Fabricators

Enginehouse

General Electric

Square D

Co-op produce market

ony & Co.

TOFC

REITH YARD

36

38

Depot

Freight

Gray Mfg.   Pendleton Grain Co-op   Pendleton Woolen Mills

TRACK ARRANGEMENT BELOW PILOT ROCK

36½

Up to LaGrande

36½

D

Down from LaGrande

C₁

39

Up to LaGrande

38

To Enterprise

E

36

C₁

A

40½

C

B

37

To Pendleton

TRACK ARRANGEMENT BELOW LAGRANDE

F

36

37

38

Branch to Joseph

40

H

G

39

To LaGrande

36

38

36

37

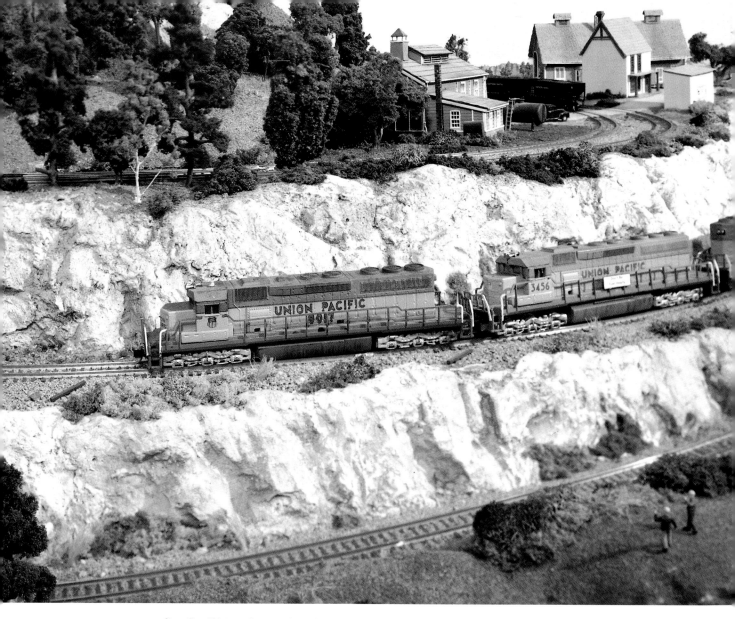

Con-Cor SD40-2s lug a unit train of soda ash through an S curve and up the 2.5 percent grade to the summit at Meacham. The real railroad and highway run parallel for several miles

Operation night on the UPN is a busy time. The timetable provides for 20 trains in a 3-hour session run with a fast clock (8:1 ratio) to represent a 24-hour day. This has proved to be a reasonable schedule that does not overwork the yards. Experience has shown that when one or more yards become overtaxed it becomes virtually impossible to maintain the timetable.

Each train on the timetable has a card that describes its itinerary and normally assigned motive power. This has proved to be a great aid to all operators and permits an operator unfamiliar with a yard or the layout to quickly understand what must be done.

Summing it up

Building the UPN has been one enormous learning experience. Researching the prototype has taught me much about the Union Pacific and the development of railroads in general. I have also experimented with and learned a number of new scenery and model building techniques and discovered that operating on a well-thought-out model railroad is as much fun — if not more so — than building the layout in the first place.

My advice to anyone just beginning a layout is to be patient. It's a good deal easier to change things on paper than after the benchwork, track, and scenery have been constructed.

All in all, I am reasonably satisfied with the UPN and my personal blend of imagineering and prototype modeling. The layout runs well, is fun to operate, and has been a source of countless hours of enjoyment.

Suppliers and organizations

When writing for information be sure to include a self-addressed, stamped envelope. Some firms offer free catalogs or literature; others charge for their catalogs. Some model railroad suppliers will sell direct to consumers; others sell only through hobby shops. Always check your local hobby shop before attempting to order direct from the manufacturer or importer. If you don't have a hobby shop in your area, most N scale products can be purchased from mail order houses. Two big ones are listed below — William K. Walthers and Con-Cor International. Both firms offer catalogs (not free) that are handy reference books showing most products offered in N scale.

American Art Clay Co., Inc.
4717 West 16th Street
Indianapolis, IN 46222
Sculpta-Mold (scenery material)

Atlas Tool Co.
378 Florence Avenue
Hillside, NJ 07205
Complete line of N scale products including locomotives, cars, track, and electrical components

Bachmann Industries, Inc.
1400 East Erie Avenue
Philadelphia, PA 19124
Complete line of N scale products including locomotives, cars, track, and structures

Blue Ribbon Models
P. O. Box 888
Marblehead, MA 01945
Rock molds, scenery materials

Bowser Mfg. Co., Inc.
21 Howard Street
Montoursville, PA 17754-0322
Turntable

Campbell Scale Models
P. O. Box 121
Tustin, CA 92680
Wood structure kits

Chooch Enterprises
P. O. Box 217
Redmond, WA 98052
Tunnel portals, retaining walls, and structures

CTT, Inc.
109 Medallion Center
Dallas, TX 75214
Track planning template, 1" = 1'

Con-Cor International
Box 328
Bensenville, IL 60106
Complete line of N scale products. Manufacturer, importer and distributor. It publishes a catalog called *Trainalog*, which lists all HO and N scale products it carries. Write for current catalog price.

Gold Rush Models
2634 Bryant Avenue South
Minneapolis, MN 55408
Offers several kits for static narrow gauge locomotives. These kits can be used with Marklin Z scale mechanisms for operating Nn3 locomotives.

Highball Products Co.
P. O. Box 43276
Cincinnati, OH 45243-0276
Ballast

Kadee Quality Products Co.
720 Grape Street
Medford, OR 97501
Operating knuckle couplers, freight cars in both standard and narrow gauge

Kato U. S. A., Inc.
415 West Golf Road, Suite 18
Arlington Heights, IL 60005
Japanese manufacturer of N scale products. Offers U. S. prototype locomotives under its own name and makes locomotives for other companies as well. Also sells line of track with ballast molded in called Unitrack.

Life-Like Products, Inc.
1600 Union Avenue
Baltimore, MD 21211
Complete line of N scale locomotives, cars, track, structures, and accessories

Micro Engineering Company
1120 Eagle Road
Fenton, MO 63026
Structure kits, flexible track, rail, ties, gauges, and tools

Model Die Casting, Inc.
3811 West Rosecrans Boulevard
P. O. Box 926
Hawthorne, CA 90251
Freight cars

MODEL RAILROADER Magazine
21027 Crossroads Circle
P. O. Box 1612
Waukesha, WI 53187
Leading model railroad magazine

Model Power
180 Smith Street
Farmingdale, NY 11735
N scale locomotives, track, and structures

Model Rectifier Corp. (MRC)
P. O. Box 267
Edison, NJ 08818
Power packs

National Model Railroad Association (NMRA)
4121 Cromwell Road
Chattanooga, TN 37421
International association of model railroad hobbyists. Organization sets industry standards, publishes a monthly magazine, and sponsors local meets, regional and national conventions. Write for current annual membership fee.

N. J. International
77 West Nicholai Street
Hicksville, NY 11801
Railroad signals, scenery supplies

NorthWest Short Line
Box 423
Seattle, WA 98111
Motors, gears, special tools

Ntrak
c/o Jim FitzGerald
2424 Alturas Road
Atascadero, CA 93422
Informal organization that establishes standards for Ntrak modules. Publishes a bimonthly newsletter, Ntrak manual, and track-planning template. Write for current newsletter subscription rate and prices of other items.

Plastruct
1020 South Wallace Place
City of Industry, CA 91748
Variety of styrene plastic sheets, strips, and shapes, plus trees

Precision Masters, Inc.
P. O. Box 28094
Lakewood, CO 80228
Car kits, couplers, and wheel sets

Rail Craft
(See Micro Engineering)

Tru-Scale Models, Inc.
P. O. Box 2258
Little Rock, AR 72203

William K. Walthers, Inc.
P. O. Box 18676,
Milwaukee, WI 53218
Major manufacturer and distributor of model railroad products in all major scales. Publishes a catalog and reference manual, "The World of N & Z Scale," which lists most products offered.

Woodland Scenics
P. O. Box 98
Linn Creek, MO 65052
Ground foam scenery supplies, tree and structure kits

Learn the lingo

AAR: Association of American Railroads, the trade association that represents the common interests of the railroad industry in such areas as standards, public relations, and advertising.

ACI: automatic car identification; see Kar Trak.

Articulated: a steam locomotive with two engines (i.e., cylinders, rods, and wheels) under one boiler.

Bad order: defective, out of order.

Big hole: an emergency stop.

Big hook: wrecking crane.

Boomer: an experienced railroad man who moves from railroad to railroad.

Block: a section of track.

Block signal: a signal at the entrance to a block indicating whether the block is occupied by a train.

Bolster: the crosswise member of the frame of a car at the truck (body bolster) or the crosswise piece at the center of a truck (truck bolster).

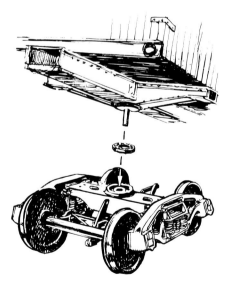

Branch line: secondary line of a railroad.

Brass (also brass hat, brass collar): railroad executives and officials.

Cab-forward: an articulated steam locomotive peculiar to the Southern Pacific, built with the cab in front for visibility in tunnels and snowsheds.

Caboose: the car that carries the crew of a freight train. It's almost always at the rear of the train. Slang terms for the caboose include buggy, bouncer, bobber, cabin, cage, crummy, hack, palace, and way car.

Camelback: a type of steam locomotive with the cab astride the boiler. The Camelback was a solution to the problem of forward visibility past the wide firebox required for burning anthracite.

Catenary: overhead trolley wire system for locomotives and cars that use pantographs for current collection.

Class I railroad: a railroad with 5 million dollars or more in annual operating revenues. Class II railroads have revenues less than 5 million dollars per year. The third classification is Switching and Terminal Railroads.

Classification lights: lights on the front of the locomotive that indicate the type of train. White lights show that the train is an extra, and green indicates that another section of the train is following.

Clear board: green or proceed signal.

Climax: a type of geared steam locomotive used primarily by logging railroads. The two cylinders drive a jackshaft parallel with the axles. Power is transmitted to each truck through bevel gears and a driveshaft; rods couple the axles on each truck. See also Shay and Heisler.

Coaling station: a structure for storing coal and transferring it into locomotive tenders.

Consist: the cars which make up a train; also a list of those cars.

Continuous rail (also welded rail, ribbonrail): rails which have been welded together to form a single rail hundreds of feet long, eliminating most rail joints, which are the weakest part of the track.

Cornfield meet: a meet out in the cornfields away from the station and the passing siding — i.e., a head-on collision.

Covered wagon: a diesel cab unit, A or B, as opposed to a hood unit.

Cowl unit: a diesel unit that looks like a cab unit but differs structurally in that the carbody is merely a full-width hood rather than a structural part of the unit.

Crossing: a track arrangement that permits two tracks to cross but does not allow trains to move from one track to the other.

Crossover: two turnouts arranged back-to-back to allow trains to move from one track to another.

CTC: Centralized Traffic Control, the direct control of all turnouts and signals on a stretch of railroad by a single dispatcher.

Cut: roadbed below the level of the surrounding terrain.

Cut of cars: a number of cars coupled together. The addition of marker lamps makes the cut of cars a train.

Deadhead: a car or train, usually passenger, moving empty; a passenger traveling on a pass. Empty freight cars are referred to as empties.

Decal: a type of lettering material for models. The letters and numbers are printed on specially prepared paper and then coated with varnish. The lettering is applied by soaking the decal in water to dissolve the film between the ink and the paper, and placing the layer of varnish and ink on the car.

Derail: a device placed over the rail to prevent a car from rolling from a siding, for example, onto a main line.

Division: a portion of a railroad considered as an operational and administrative unit.

Doubleheader: a train pulled by two locomotives, each with an engine crew, as opposed to diesel or electric locomotive units operating in multiple as a single locomotive with one crew.

Doubling a hill: splitting a train and taking it up a steep grade in two parts, one at a time.

Draft gear: the mechanism which connects the coupler to the frame of the car. In the model world, the coupler mounting box is sometimes called the draft gear.

Drawbar: any coupling, either a solid bar or couplers, between two pieces of rolling stock.

Dry transfer: a lettering process in which the letter itself is a thin plastic film with a pressure-sensitive wax adhesive.

Enginehouse: a building in which locomotives are serviced.

Extra: a train not authorized by a timetable schedule.

Fill: roadbed built up above the surrounding terrain.

Flange: the part of the wheel which runs below and inside the top of the rails to guide the wheel.

Gandy dancer: a track worker.

Gas-electric: a self-propelled car powered by a gasoline engine driving a generator which supplies current to motors on the axles. Gas-electrics were the common form of branchline passenger train in the 1920's and 1930's.

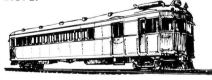

Glad hand: the metal coupling on the end of an air hose.

Grab iron: handholds on the sides, ends, and roofs of cars.

Head-end cars: mail, baggage, and express cars, usually run at the front of a passenger train.

Heisler: a type of geared steam locomotive used by logging railroads. It had two cylinders arranged in a V connected to a driveshaft which in turn was connected to the trucks. See also Climax and Shay.

Highball: a proceed signal.

Hood unit: a road-switcher, so called because of the construction of the locomotive, with the machinery covered by a hood rather than a full-width cab.

Hy-cube: a modern type of box car that is taller than standard and thus has a higher cubic capacity.

Helper: a locomotive added to a train to help it climb a grade.

High iron: the main line.

Hog: a locomotive.

Hogger: an engineer.

Hostler: a workman who services locomotives between runs.

Hotbox: an axle bearing that has become hot because of lack of lubrication.

Interchange: a junction of two railroads where cars are transferred from one line to the other.

Interlocking: a mechanical or electrical system of signaling that ensures that only one train at a time is allowed to move through a junction.

ICC: the Interstate Commerce Commission, an agency of the Federal government that regulates most forms of surface transportation. Among its powers are the approval of both instituting and discontinuing railroad service.

Interurban: an electrically operated light railway between cities and towns, as opposed to local streetcar service.

In the hole: in a siding to meet or pass another train.

Johnson bar: the manual reversing lever of older steam locomotives.

Journal: the load-bearing part of an axle. The weight of the axle is carried by the journal bearing, which is enclosed by the journal box.

Kar Trak: a modern system used to keep track of all railroad equipment.

It employs ACI (automatic car identification) reflective labels on all rolling stock, trackside scanners, and computers.

Kingpin: the pivot on which a truck swivels. Center pin is the more common term for the prototype.

Kitbash: to combine parts from kits to produce a model unlike the straight kit models.

LCL: Less than Carload Lot, any shipment of freight too small to fill an entire car.

Main line: any of the principal, heavy-traffic lines of a railroad.

Maintenance-of-way equipment: the machinery and rolling stock used to keep track and roadbed in good condition.

Markers: lamps hung on the rear of the last car of the train to show that the cars are indeed a train and to indicate its status. Often nowadays substitutes are used, such as reflectors or a red flag jammed into the coupler. Similar lamps on the front of the locomotive are called classification lamps.

M.U.: multiple unit, a method of controlling several diesel units, electric cars, or locomotives from one cab. M.U. cars are electric passenger cars for operation on electrified portions of a steam or diesel railroad, as in a suburban district. Interurbans, subway cars, and RDC's are technically M.U. cars, but the term is reserved for steam-road electric cars.

Muzzle-loader: a hand-fired steam engine, i.e., one without a mechanical stoker.

Narrow gauge: track with a gauge less than 4 feet 8½ inches.

On the advertised: on time.

Pantograph: a current pickup device resembling a folding clotheshorse for electric locomotives and cars.

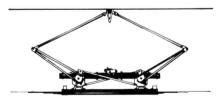

Piggyback: the movement of truck trailers on flat cars. Also called TOFC.

Pullman: a sleeping car or parlor car operated by the Pullman Company.

Pull the pin: operate the uncoupling lever.

Rail Diesel Car (RDC): a self-propelled diesel-powered passenger car built by the Budd Company.

Railfan: a person who enjoys riding, watching, photographing, and reading about trains.

Reefer: a refrigerator car.

Red board: a signal indicating stop.

Right of way: the track, roadbed, and property along the track owned by the railroad.

Rip track: the track in a yard where minor car repairs are done.

Road-switcher: a general-purpose diesel that can be used for both yard switching and road duties. They are also called hood units.

Roundhouse: an enginehouse like a sector of a circle in shape, and usually surrounding a turntable.

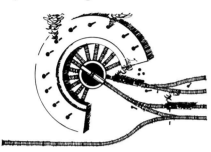

Runaround: a switching maneuver in which the locomotive uncouples from its train, pulls ahead, backs past on an adjacent track, and moves forward to couple onto the rear of the train; also the track itself where the move takes place.

Saw-by: a maneuver by which two trains can meet at a siding which is too short to hold either.

Schedule: that portion of a timetable that lists the class, direction, number, and movement of regular trains.

Shay: a type of geared steam locomotive used extensively in logging. It had three cylinders mounted vertically on the right side of the boiler driving a crankshaft geared to all the axles.

Shoo-fly: a temporary track laid around an obstruction.

Short line: a small railroad, generally Class II.

Slip switch: a piece of trackwork that combines a crossing and four turnouts to permit trains to move from one track to the other or to simply stay on the same track.

Slug: a weighted locomotive unit with traction motors but no diesel engine or generator. It is used in conjunction with a diesel locomotive for additional tractive force.

Smokejack: a chimney on a car or building.

Snowshed: a structure built over the track in mountainous areas to protect the tracks from snow.

Spot a car: to place a car in its designated position, as at an industry or on a station track.

Spring switch: a turnout held in one position by a spring so that facing-point traffic always takes the same route but trailing-point traffic can run through the turnout from either track.

Superelevation: the raising of the outer rail on a curve; banking.

Talgo: a type of lightweight passenger train built by American Car & Foundry. In the model world the term is applied to truck-mounted couplers.

Tangent: straight track.

Tank engine: a steam locomotive that carries its fuel and water supply in tanks hung over or alongside the boiler or on a frame extension at the rear instead of in a tender.

Tender: a car, attached to a steam locomotive, that carries extra fuel and water for the locomotive.

Throttle: the speed control of the locomotive; in the model world, a rheostat, variable transformer, or other speed controller.

Timetable: the authority for the movement of regular trains subject to the railroad's operating rules.

Ton-mile: one ton of freight moved one mile.

Traction: public utility transportation; by extension, all electrically operated trains.

Transition curve: a section of track with a gradually diminishing radius between the straight track and the circular part of the curve. Also called a spiral.

Turnout: track switch.

Turntable: a rotating bridge used for turning locomotives.

Unit: a diesel locomotive unit.

Unit train: a freight train that carries a single commodity from source to destination and returns empty.

USRA: United States Railroad Administration. The USRA was responsible for the operation of the country's railroads during World War I.

Varnish: a passenger train. Wooden passenger cars used to be given many coats of varnish.

Vestibule: the enclosed area at the end of a passenger car where the side doors are located. Early passenger cars had only an open platform. Around the 1890's narrow-vestibule cars came into use, with a vestibule only as wide as the passageway between the cars. The full-width vestibule followed soon after.

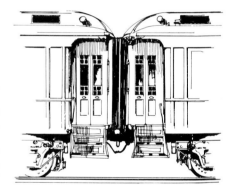

Water column: a standpipe adjacent to the track and connected to a water supply for filling steam locomotive tenders.

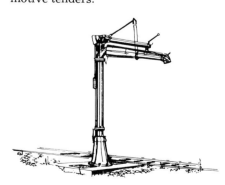

Wye: a track configuration for turning a locomotive or a train or for joining a branch to a main line for operation in both directions.

Yard engine (also yard goat): a switching locomotive.

Index

N scale has a bright future

The year 1990 marked the 25th anniversary of N scale modeling in America. A betting man in 1965 might reasonably have wagered that by 1990 N would be the majority scale in the United States. That has certainly happened in Japan, but not elsewhere around the world. In the United States, N scale quickly captured about 13 percent of the market and then just remained there. But in the last five years we have seen some real growth in the popularity of N scale.

Between 1983 and 1988 the popularity of N scale increased from 13.4 percent or 30,000 modelers to 16 percent or 39,500. That's a 30 percent increase in 5 years! What's even more remarkable is the fact that in the same 5-year span those who model in N scale as a secondary scale have increased from 24,000 (10.6 percent) to 64,000 (26 percent).

Why didn't N take the model railroad hobby by storm 25 years ago? In part it's because N scale was looked upon as toylike by "serious" model railroaders when introduced. The European manufacturers assumed they had to go with high rail (code 80) and deep flanges (0.35″) for reliable operation. Since then those assumptions have been proven wrong. Flange depths of .20″ are now standard, and reliably operating layouts have been built with rail as small as code 40.

Another drawback was spotty locomotive performance even by engines with the same brand name. A few ran great, many were mediocre, and some were just plain lousy. That's changed dramatically for the better in recent years.

With the toylike stigma behind it and with living space becoming increasingly expensive, N scale's popularity should surge throughout the 1990s. It's a modeling scale with a bright future.